Look

A Comprehensive Equine Glossary

Meanings • Phonetic Pronunciation • Cross-referencing
for over 2,000 words pertaining to horses, horse-related
activities, and equine veterinary medicine

Researched, Compiled & Edited by
Equine Graphics™ Publishing

SmallHorse™ Press & Productions
Post Office Box 8016
Zanesville, OH   43702-8016
800-375-9378

Editor's Comments

This publication represents several years of research and compilation of hundreds of words used in the horse industry. What started out to be a simple reference source for the layperson has evolved into a larger work encompassing the wide variety of colloquial, regional, geographical, and discipline preferences of horsepeople in the United States. It has become apparent that this glossary will be an on-going work, as more fine-tuning of expressions and word meanings is accomplished. Through research of respected equine publications and the reviews of knowledgable equine professionals around the country, *Look It Up* will continue to grow and remain a reliable source for equine-related word usage.

Acknowledgments

Many thanks to those who devoted time taken from busy schedules to review the book and make suggestions, additions, and/or corrections:

Kenneth Marcella, D.V.M., equine veterinarian & writer, Suwanee, GA.
Jerry Hull, avid horseman & owner of Trophy Tack, Bixby, OK.
Barbara Naviaux, Miniature Horse breeder, student of genetics, & author, Placerville, CA.
Candace Morasch, Morgan Horse breeder and Speech-Language Pathologist, Williams, OR.
Bob Burdekin, Master Farrier, Phoenix, OR
Carole A. Baker, Equine Studies Program, Teikyo Post University, Waterbury, CT
Connie Owens, editor of The Illinois Horse Network newspaper, Sorento, IL
Bonnie Kreitler, equine journalist and photographer, Fairfield, CT.
Lynn Ingles, long-time Morgan Horse and Miniature Horse breeder, Sorento, IL.

Disclaimer

A

AI—see **artificial insemination**
AV—see **artificial vagina**
a halt—a stop.
"above the bit"—when the horse raises and stretches its head forward, having its mouth higher than the rider's hands.
abraded [*uh-bray´-ded*]—(*v*) scraped or "skinned"
abscess [*ab´-sess*]—(*n*) an inflamed, swollen area in which pus collects.
absorption (also "resorption" or "reabsorption")—when a mare absorbs a dead fetus back into her system.
accessory sex glands—glands in the stallion's reproductive tract that add secretions to the seminal fluid.
"account for"—(*v*) in foxhunting, the term for killing a fox.
"Acey Deucy"—in racing, riding with one stirrup leather longer than the other; used to keep balance on sharp turns.
acquired immunity—disease resistance acquired from immunization.
acquired trait—a trait resulting from a response to environment; not inherited.
acre—unit measure for land: 1 acre=4,840 sq. yds or 43,560 sq. ft.
accreditation (also "certification")—a "license" to provide instruction or training, usu ally acquired through specific courses given by the certifying organization.
"across the board"—in racing, a bet on a horse to win, place, and show.
Acting Master—in hunting, the person appointed on a temporary basis to organize hunts
action—the way a horse moves through the gaits.
acupressure—using pressure rather than needle stimulation on the acupuncture points of the body.
acupuncture—the ancient practice of inserting needles along certain lines (meridians) on the body as a method of curing disease or relieving pain.
acute—of short duration; not chronic.
adaptation—adjusting to changes in the environment.
adenovirus—a virus that causes respiratory disease.
adhesion—firm, fibrous attachment between two structures.
adrenalin (*epinephrine*)—hormone produced by the adrenal gland; it increases blood pressure, speeds up heart rate, slows digestion.
adult—in showing, the term for an exhibitor that is 18 years or older; (this can vary slightly depending upon the sanctioning organization.)
affinity—close relationship.
afterbirth (see also **placenta**)—expelled placenta.
"against the clock"—a competition or jump-off that is judged by time.
agalactia [*ay-guh-lak´-tee-uh*]—the absence of milk after foaling.
aged—a horse nine years or older.
agent—one who acts as a spokesperson for a stable or owner; one who has the power to buy or sell horses, or manage business transactions.
aids—signals used by the rider to give instructions to the horse; **artificial a.**-used to reinforce the natural aids; includes spurs, crop, etc.; **natural a.**-a part of the body, such as the legs, voice, weight, or hands used to signal the horse.
"airs above the ground"—see **"high school airs"**
albino—a horse with a pure white coat accompanied by blue or pink eyes; sometimes the result of genetic mutation.
alfalfa—a legume used for hay; it is high in protein and calcium.
"all around cow horse"—a horse that is trained to do everything a cowboy needs to perform his job.
"all on"—in hunting, the term used to indicate that all the hounds are up with the pack.
all out—in racing, when a horse extends itself to the fullest.

allele [*uh-leel'*]—the mutation of a gene to another form.

allergic—hypersensitive to a specific substance.

"also-ran"—in racing, a horse that does not place in a race.

alter—see **geld**

amateur—a person whose avocation is showing or exhibiting horses for enjoyment and prizes, and for which that person receives no payment.

amble—a slow gait in which the horse's hind and foreleg on the same side move forward together in two time.

amino acid—organic building blocks for protein that are important in metabolism.

amnion [*am'-nee-on*]—the fluid-filled membrane surrounding a fetus, acting as a protective cushion.

anaerobic [*an-er-oh'-bik*]—living without air or oxygen.

analgesic [*an-ul-gee'-zik*]—pain killer.

anaphylaxis [*anna-fill-ax'-sys*]—an exaggerated allergic reaction to a substance.

ancestor—an individual from which another individual is descended, such as a parent or grandparent.

anemia—a condition in which there is a reduction of the number of red blood corpuscles or the total amount of hemoglobin in the blood, resulting in lack of vigor or vitality.

anestrus [*an-es'-trus*]—time during the year when a mare does not normally cycle.

anhydrosis [*an-high-droh'-sys*]—inability to sweat.

ankle boot—see **boots**

anklet—see **sock**

ankylosed [*ank'-kel-ohst*] *(also "dry joint")*—fused or joined joints or fibrous parts.

anorexia [*an-or-rex'-see-uh*]—lack of appetite for food.

anoxia [*an-ox'-see-uh*]—absence of oxygen in the blood or tissues.

"ante-post betting"—in racing, placing bets at an agreed price before the day of a race.

anterior—pertaining to the front part of the body.

anthelmintic [*an-thel-mint'-ik*]—a dewormer medicine used for control of intestinal worms.

antibiotic—destroying or inhibiting the growth of bacteria.

antibody—a protein produced in the body in response to contact with an antigen; this protein can neutralize the antigen and create immunity.

anti-cast surcingle—a surcingle having a metal arch that sits above the withers; this device prevents the horse from rolling and becoming cast in the stall.

antigen [*an'-ti-jen*]—protein substance that the body recognizes as being foreign; when present, the body produces a specific antibody against the antigen.

antihistamine—a drug that reduces the effects of histamine in allergic reaction.

antiseptic—preventing infection.

anus—the external opening of the rectum.

anvil—a heavy iron block on which horseshoes are shaped.

aorta [*ay-or'-tuh*]—the major artery that carries blood away from the heart.

appointment card (also "fixture")—in foxhunting, the notification of time, date and place of upcoming meets.

appointments—term used to describe the various equipment or tack used for horses, as well as the uniform, livery, or attire of the rider or driver.

apprentice (also "bug")—in racing, a rider who has not ridden a certain number of winners within a specified period of time.

approved—see **sanctioned**

apron—1) the protective covering worn by farriers while shoeing horses; usually made of strong hide; 2) in racing, the paved surface between the stands and the racetrack.

arenacraft—in showing, the art of showing off the horse's ability to its fullest.

arena—the area in which a horseshow or event is held; also, the area where a horse is trained or worked.

artery—a blood vessel that carries blood away from the heart.

arthritis—inflammation of the joints.

arthroscope—an instrument used for viewing areas inside a joint, sometimes attached to a video camera.

articular cartilage [*ar-tih´-kew-lur*]—the cartilage covering the ends of the bones that meet at a joint.

artificial aid—see **aids**

artificial insemination (AI)—a procedure where semen is placed in the mare's vagina by a veterinarian; the stallion never physically breeds the mare.

artificial selection (also "culling")—careful breed management by man to improve or remove certain characteristics, as opposed to natural selection.

artificial vagina (AV)—a device used for collecting semen from the stallion.

"as hounds ran"—the distance covered by the hounds in a hunt.

ascarids [*ass´-kar-ids*] (also "roundworms")—serious intestinal parasites in young horses.

Aschheim-Zondek test [*ash-hime-zon´-deck*]—used for pregnancy tests in mares.

"asking the question"—in racing, show-jumping, or combined training, the request by the rider for the horse to make a tremendous effort, even when it is being pushed to the limits.

aspirate [*ass´-per-ate*]—(*v*) to remove by suction a gas or fluid from a body cavity; [*ass´-per-it*] (*n*) a sample of gas or fluid removed from the body cavity.

aspiration—1) removal by suction; 2) the act of sucking fluid into the lungs.

assay—analysis.

astringent—a preparation that contracts body tissue and checks secretions.

asymmetry—uneveness.

asymptomatic—without symptoms.

ataxia [*ay-tax´-see-uh*]—incoordination due to loss of muscular control or possible nervous system disease.

"at bay"—in hunting, the position of the hounds when keeping off the quarry.

"at the canter"—three hoofbeats heard, with a moment of suspension when all four hooves are off the ground.

"at the trot"—two hoofbeats heard, legs moving in alternate diagonal pairs; hoofbeats separated by a moment of suspension: right fore and left hind feet together, then left fore and right hind feet together.

"at the walk"—four hoofbeats heard at equal intervals: left hindfoot, left forefoot, right hindfoot, right forefoot.

atresia [*uh-tree´-zhuh*]—absence of a normal opening.

atresia coli [*uh-tree´-zhuh koh´-lye*]—congenital closure of the intestine.

atrophy [*a´-troh-fee*]—wasting away of a body part or tissue.

Australian saddle—see **saddle, English**

autogenous [*aw-tah´-jen-us*]—produced in or by an animal's own body.

average earnings index—in racing, an index used to compare stallions; the average earnings of the progeny of the considered stallion are divided by the total average earnings of all the starters.

azoturia [*ah-zoe-ter´-ee-uh*] (also "Monday-morning sickness")—a "day off" affliction mainly of workhorses or high performance horses that are heavily grained to sustain energy, when allowed to rest for a day before returning to work, overproduction of lactic acid causes tying-up, rigidity, sweating, and possible death if not treated.

 B

back—1) the command to move backwards in a straight line; 2) to place a bet on a horse; 3) the part of the horse's body between the withers and the loin.

"back at the knee"—British term for conformation fault where the knee is behind the vertical, causing strain.

back hander—in polo, when the player is traveling forward and hits the ball backwards.

back jockey—the stop skirt on a western saddle.

back pad—the saddle portion of a harness.

back strap—on harness, a strap that runs from the saddle back to the crupper and helps to keep the saddle positioned properly, as well as holding the hip strap.

backcross—crossing a progeny with one of the parents, or with another horse of the same genotype.

backer—the person placing a bet on a horse.

backstretch—in racing, the straightaway between turns on the far side of the track.

bacteria—microorganisms of the class *Schizomycetes* that can be beneficial or harmful.

bactericide—a bacteria-destroying agent.

bacterin—a suspension of bacteria killed by heat or chemical means.

bag—see **udder**

bag up—term used to describe the mare's udder as it begins to enlarge prior to foaling.

bag fox—a fox kept in captivitiy temporarily until it is required for a hunt.

balance—when the horse has good rhythm, takes even strides, remains on the bit and "in frame."

baldface—a white face marking covering one or both eyes and extending toward the nose.

balding girth—a girth composed of three pieces, two of which are twisted; designed to prevent slippage of the saddle on a horse with a badly shaped belly (British); also prevents chafing behind the elbows.

balk (also "refusal")—to refuse to perform a maneuver or obey instruction.

balling gun—a device used for "shooting" medicine into the back of the horse's mouth, preventing it from spitting it out.

Ballotade [*bal´-oh-todd*]—an "air above the ground" in which the horse rears, then jumps forward and draws the hind legs up below the quarters, then lands on all four legs.

ballottement [*ba-lot´-mint*]—a pregnancy diagnosis procedure where the uterine wall is tapped via the rectum, and the fetus, if present, is felt to bounce back against the wall.

balm—a rubifacient in cream form that is used to increase heat and promote vasodilatation; a balm usually contains one or more essential oils that produce a tingling effect on the skin

band (also "herd")—a group of horses.

bandy legs—see **bow legs**

banged—tail trimming worn by hunter-type horses; the long hair of the tail is cut with scissors straight across in a blunt cut, the ends even with the hocks.

bang-tail—in racing, a slang term for a horse.

bar shoe—a horseshoe that has a closed back that supports the frog and heel of the hoof; used for horses with quarter cracks or bruises; **Hart b.**-a shoe used for feet affected by founder.

bareback riding—riding a horse without saddle or blanket.

barker foal—see **Convulsive Foal Syndrome**

barn (also "stable" "shedrow")—a building used for housing livestock; a horse barn is usually constructed differently than a dairy barn.

barn blind—common term describing the inability of horse owners to recognize faults or poor breeding decisions in their stock.

barn-sour—term used to describe a horse that resists leaving the barn area when being asked to work, or one that consistently wants to head back to the barn when being worked out in the field, arena, or trail.

barrage—a jump-off.

barrel—the thickest part of the horse's girth, containing the chest and rib cage.

barren—a mare that fails to become pregnant over time.

barrier—1) the point at which a race starts; 2) in rodeo, the point behind which the roper or steer wrestler waits until the stock is out of the chute.

bars—1) in the horse's mouth, the gap in the lower jaw between the molar and incisor teeth, where the bit lies; 2) in the foot, the area along each side of the frog.

Bartholin's glands [*bar´-thoh-linz*]—glands that lubricate the posterior portion of the mare's reproductive tract.

base narrow—greater distance between the horse's legs at the top than at the bottom when standing square; a conformation fault.

base wide—greater distance between the horse's legs at the bottom than at the top when standing square; a conformation fault. · ·

"base-wide with cow hocks"—conformation fault where the distance between the feet is wider than the distance between the hocks when standing square.

bastard strangles—strangles resulting in abscesses of lymph nodes anywhere in the body other than the throat and submandibular area.

bat—see **crop**

bay—a horse with a brown coat over dark skin, black points (mane, tail, & lower legs).

bearing rein (also "check rein")—the rein that applies pressure on the side of the neck as well as pulling sideways and backwards on the bit.

"behind the bit" (see also **overbent**)—the horse draws its head back away from contact with the bit in an effort to evade its action.

bell boot—a rubber bell-shaped cuff that fits over the foot and hoof to protect them from damage while working.

belly band—the girth strap that secures the backpad of a harness.

bench knees—term for offset cannon bones that are not directly under the forearm.

benign [*bee-nine´*]—doing little or no harm.

bib (also "cradle")—a collar-like device fastened under the horse's jaw to prevent licking or chewing itself.

bib martingale—see **martingale**

"big lick"—in showing, the term for the total overall high action of a shod-up Tennessee Walking Horse.

"big lick horse" (also "open horse" "stake horse")—in showing, reference to a Tennessee Walking Horse with action enhanced by maximum pad and hoof length.

bight [*bite*]—1) the loop or slack part of a rope; 2) the ends (behind the rider's hands) of a set of closed reins.

bike—a two-wheeled racing vehicle.

bilateral—pertaining to two sides; on both side.

billet—1) the three straps on an English saddle, located under the skirt, to which the girth attaches; 2) the straps on a western saddle that attach the rear or flank cinch.

binocular vision—viewing an area with both eyes.

biochemical—pertaining to the chemical processes of living organisms.

biopsy—1)(*v*) removal of tissue from living organisms for diagnostic examination; 2) (*n*) a sample obtained by biopsy.

birth canal—the uterus, cervix, vagina, and vulva; the passageway from the uterus to the outside.

bit—the part of a bridle that controls the horse, consisting of a metal bar in the mouth attached to the reins.

bit and bradoon—see **Weymouth bit**

bitch fox—in hunting, a female fox.

bitch hound—in hunting, a female hound.

bite—term describing the way a horse's teeth come together.

bitless bridle—bridles used without bits, pressure being exerted on the nose and the curb groove instead of the mouth; a hackamore is a bitless bridle.

bitting harness (also "bitting rig")—training aid used to teach the horse how to position and hold its head.

black—a solid black color haircoat; can have white markings.

black saddler—the maker of driving harness, rather than riding tack.

blacksmith (see also **farrier**)—an artisan who works with iron; one who makes horseshoes.

blanket—1) *(n)* a heavy, insulated winter covering; 2) the term to describe the distribution area of spots on an appaloosa's rump; 3) *(v)* to cover a horse with a blanket.

blaze—a white face marking that begins on the forehead and extends down the face and nose.

bleeder—a horse that bleeds from the nose; most bleeds are of lung origin, not true "nosebleeds."

blemish—any scar left by an injury or wound; sometimes congenital.

blind bucker—a horse that bucks indiscriminately.

blind spavin—see occult spavin

blinkers (also "blinker cups")—eye-shields on harness or bridle, used to keep a horse from looking anywhere except where it is headed.

blister—a counter-irritant that is extremely irritating and causes some degree of skin reaction from light redness to blistering.

Blood Horse—an English Thoroughbred.

blood poisoning—see septicemia

bloodstock—Thoroughbred horses, especially racing and breeding animals.

bloodstock agent—one who represents a buyer or seller of Thoroughbreds at private sale or public auction.

blood-typing—a method of verifying the parentage of a horse; some breed registries require blood-typing before registration will be executed.

bloodworms—see strongyles

"blow a stirrup"—to lose a stirrup iron.

"blow away"—in hunting, blowing a signal on a hunting horn to send the hounds out after a fox.

"blow out"—in racing, a short, timed workout for the purpose of sharpening the horse's speed.

"blow up"—1) in showing, when a horse breaks or misbehaves; 2) (also "boil over") to start bucking.

board—1) *(v)* to pay for stabling a horse at a public or private barn; 2) *(n)* the fee paid for stabling a horse; 3) in racing, short for the "tote board" where odds and other information are displayed.

body brush—medium-stiff bristled brush used for removing dust & hair.

body clip—to shear the horse's entire hair coat very closely.

body roller—see surcingle

bog rider—a cowboy who rescues cattle trapped in marshland or mud.

bog spavin—swelling of the capsule around the hock joint; caused by strain; considered a blemish.

"boil over" (also "blow up")—to start bucking.

bolt—*(v)* 1) to suddenly run off, out of control; 2) to veer away from a straight course.

bonding—the crucial relationship development between mare and foal.

bone spavin (also "Jack spavin" "high spavin")—serious arthritis in the bones of the hock, causing calcium deposits and swelling on the inside; considered to be an unsoundness rather than a blemish.

book—1) *(v)* to reserve a breeding to a stallion; 2) *(n)* a stallion's "book" or reservation sheet; 3) in racing, a jockey's "book," or riding commitments.

bookie—a slang term for bookmaker.

bookmaker—a professional betting man, licensed to accept bets placed by others.

booster—a regularly-repeated immunization that restores or increases the amount of immunity in the body.

boots—protective devices of many varieties; **ankle b.** (also "brushing b.")-protect the hind and front feet from brushing the inside ankles; **bell b.**-prevent damage while working; **galloping b.**-protect ankles, shins, and tendons; **knee b.**-protect knees while jogging or racing; **performance b.**-cover the entire foot and have a ribbed sole; **quarter b.** (also "overreach b.")-protect the quarter section of foot from overreach injury; **sesamoid b.** (also "run-down b.")-prevent stress during hard work at fast speeds; **shipping b.**-protect the legs of horses being transported; **shoe boil b.**-protect horse from damage to elbow while lying down; **skid/sliding b.**-protect hind pasterns and fetlocks; **splint b.**- cover the cannon bone area on the front legs and protect during exercise; **tendon b.**-protect the tendons by creating supporting pressure during exertion;

bosal [*bow-sahl'*]—part of a hackamore bridle consisting of a braided rawhide or rope loop around the horse's nose, at the end of the nasal bone; applies direct pressure.

"boss mare"—the dominant, most aggressive mare in a herd.

bot—the larva of the bot fly; attaches itself to the lining of the horse's stomach.

bot comb—a comb with tiny, very sharp teeth used for scraping bot eggs off the horse's hair.

bot fly—large-bodied yellow flies that lay their eggs on the hairs of the legs, shoulders, and jaw.

"both ways of the ring"—in riding or driving, moving around the arena in both directions at the instruction of the judges.

bottom line—1) the area along the underside of the horse, from behind the elbow to the flank; 2) the lower half of an extended pedigree diagram.

boundary rider—a ranch worker who rides all the fences and repairs them.

bow legs (also "bandy legs")—conformation fault in which the hocks are set too far apart, usually causing interference between the hind feet; in front, the knees deviate to the outside of the center line of the leg.

bowed tendons (see also **tendinitis**)—tendons that have taken on a bowed shape as a result of severe leg strain or improper bandaging.

boxy feet—feet with a small frog and high heel.

brace—a rubifacient that is a mixture of drugs used following work; contains high concentrations of alcohol to pull fluid out of tissues and prevent collection of fluid in tendon sheaths.

brachygnathism [*brah'-kee-nuh-thiz-um*] (also "parrot mouth" "overshot jaw" "sow mouth")—a deformity in which the upper jaw protrudes out farther than the lower.

bradoon carrier—on a Weymouth bridle, a fine leather strap, with the buckle on the right side, that goes through the browband and lies under the crownpiece.

braiding (also "plaiting")—decorative grooming technique used on the mane and forelock, and sometimes tail, of hunter and dressage horses, or for particular disciplines that allow it.

bran—a by-product of grain milling; used as a mild laxative for horses.

brand—a hairless scar left by a hot iron; used for identification marking.

break—1) (*v*) to train a young horse, usually as a yearling; 2) in racing, to leave the starting gate; 3) in showing, when a horse moves into another gait before being asked, such as from a trot to a canter.

"break maiden" ("earn a diploma")—in racing, the term for a horse or rider winning the first race of its career.

breakaway—in roping, a special rope that falls free of the animal once the loop has tightened; the animal is never tied.

breakdown—1) the laceration of the suspensory ligament and/or deep and superficial flexor tendons, or fracture of a sesamoid bone; this causes the back of the fetlock to drop to the ground; 2) any injury that has the potential to end the horse's performance career.

breaking cart—a low-built heavy cart with long shafts, used for training green horses to drive.

breaking water—a common term for the expulsion of the fluid surrounding the fetus during the first stage of labor.

break-over—the distance from the point of the heel as it leaves the ground to the toe where it leaves the ground.

breast collar—see **breastplate**

breastplate (also "breast collar" or "Dutch collar")—device attached to the saddle on harness to keep it from sliding back.

breech presentation—delivery in which the hindquarters of the foal are presented first.

breeches—tight-fitting riding pants worn for huntseat or jumping.

breechen—see **breeching**

breeching [*brih'-chen*] (also "holdback" "britching" "britchen" "breechen") the harness strap behind the horse's hind legs that acts as the brake on the load being pulled.

breed—1) (*n*) a related group of animals that show inherited characteristics that make them different than other members of the same species; 2) (*v*) to mate or copulate.

breeder—one who owns breeding animals and practices animal husbandry.

breeding chute—generally a protective "L" shaped structure used for teasing and/or breeding mares.

breeding contract—a legal and binding document or agreement between the stallion owner and the mare owner; contains detailed obligations of both parties and payment terms for services rendered.

breeding roll—a padded instrument that is placed between the mare and stallion that prevents the stallion's penis from penetrating the mare too deeply.

breeding shed—the building where all breeding takes place.

breeding stitch—a reinforcing suture placed at the lower end of a Caslick's suture line.

breeding value—assigned to a horse for a certain trait; calculated by comparing the horse to the population average.

"breeze in"—to win a race easily.

bridle (also "head-stall")—1) (*n*) the series of leather straps, reins, and metal bit which give the rider or driver control over the horse; **rolled b.**—a bridle that is made of rolled leather pieces rather than flat pieces; 2) (*v*) to put a bridle on a horse

bridle front—see **browband**

bridlepath—area directly behind the ears where the back strap of the bridle lies.

britchen—see **breeching**

britching—see **breeching**

broad ligaments—the fibrous bands of tissue that suspend the mare's reproductive tract from the upper wall of the abdominal cavity.

broad-spectrum antibiotic—a medication having a wide range of antibiotic effects against a variety of microorganisms.

broken wind—see **heaves**

bronc riding—in rodeo, a timed event where the rider uses only a leather handle on a wide leather band around the horse's middle.

bronchial—having to do with the bronchi of the respiratory system.

bronchi—the two main branches of the trachea (*singular: bronchus*).

bronco—unbroken wild horse.

bronco-buster—person who breaks and trains wild horses.

broodmare—a mare used solely for breeding purposes.

broodmare sire—the sire of the dam of a horse; term for stallion that produces good broodmares.

browband (also "bridle front")—the part of a bridle that lies across the forehead.

brown—a haircoat color that is darker than chestnut; can also be black with brown points.

brown saddler—the maker of saddles and bridles, rather than harness.

Brucella abortus [*broo-sell'-uh uh-bor'-tus*]—species of bacteria that cause abortion in mares, Bang's disease in cattle, and undulent fever in humans.

Brumby—Australian wild horse.

brush—1) (*n*) an injury from one hoof hitting the inside of the opposite leg; 2) (*v*) in racing, when two horses slightly touch each other while running; 3) in hunting, the tail of a fox;

brush box—in jumping, a fence consisting of a low box filled with greenery or shrubs.

brushing boot—see **boot, ankle**

buck—a maneuver where the horse arches its back and leaps into the air, coming back down with stiff forelegs and its head down.

buck knees—see **"over at the knee"**

buckaroo—1) a cowboy; 2) a bronco-buster.

buckaroo saddle—see **saddle, western; cowhand**

buckboard—a 4-wheeled open driving vehicle, having flexible floorboards that rest directly on the axles of the vehicle.

bucked shins—periostitis of the cannon bone (see also **periostitis**).

bucks—wooden crosspieces that are part of a pack saddle.

buckskin—a horse with a light-brown or tan coat, black points, and sometimes a black stripe along the spine (dorsal stripe).

"bug" or "bug boy"—see **apprentice**

buggy—a light 4-wheeled carriage with a single seat, drawn by one horse; in Britain, this vehicle may have two wheels.

bulbs—the two areas at the back of the foot, on either side, above the heel.

bull clip—the strong metal clip at the end of a lead rope.

bull pole—a sturdy pole attached to the halter to keep an aggressive stallion from crowding the handler.

bull riding—in rodeo, a timed event where the contestant rides a bull with a rope around its middle using only one hand.

bulldog mouth (also "undershot jaw")—see **prognathism**

bulldogging (also "steer wrestling")—in rodeo, a timed event where the contestant rides his horse alongside a loose steer, then jumps on to the head of the animal and wrestles it to the ground.

bull-nosed foot—term for a foot that has been rasped down to fit a shoe.

bumper—1) an amateur race rider; 2) an amateur race.

bush track—an unofficial race meeting (US).

bute [*bewt*]—common term for the anti-inflammatory drug, phenylbutazone.

butt rope (see also **come along**)—a long rope that is attached to the halter, then brought around behind the horse's rump and up the other side; used for training foals to lead and also for teaching horses to load onto a trailer.

buttress foot—see **pyramidal disease**

buy-back (also "RNA")—(*n*) term used for the fee paid by the consignor (seller) for a horse that did not sell for the minimum price set by the seller, thereby being taken back by the seller.

by—sired or fathered by.

"bye-day"—in hunting, an extra meet or substitute date for a meet not held.

 C

CEM—see **Contagious Equine Metritis**

CFS—see **Convulsive Foal Syndrome**

CID—see **Combined Immunodeficiency Disease**

COPD—see **Chronic Obstructive Pulmonary Disease**

cadence—beat, or measured movement.

calf-horse (also "rope horse")—a horse specially trained for calf-roping.

calf-knee—American term for *back at the knee.*

calf-roping—in rodeo, a timed event where the contestant ropes the calf from horseback, then jumps down and ties the calf by three legs.

California rein—see **romal**

calks (also "stickers")—in racing, heel projections on horseshoes that are used in adverse weather to give traction.

call judge—the judge who conducts a class.

call over—in racing, the naming of the horses in a race.

canker—a chronic dermatitis similar to thrush, but involving the whole foot; caused by poor sanitation and neglect.

cannon bone—the long bone between the knee and the fetlock joint.

canter—a gait in which the hooves strike the ground in three beat time.

cantle—the flared back part of the seat on a saddle.

cap—the visitor fee for a day's hunting.

capillaries—tiny blood vessels that connect arteries and veins.

capped hock—permanent swelling at the point of the hock as a result of direct injury; considered a blemish.

capped elbow—permanent swelling at the point of the elbow, caused by pressure of the horseshoe when the horse is lying down; considered a blemish.

Capriole [*kap-ree-ohl'*]—an "air above the ground" in which the horse half rears, jumps forward and high into the air kicking out the hind legs, soles of the feet turned up, then lands collectedly on all four legs.

carcinoma [*kar-sin-noh'-muh*]—malignant growth that spreads (metastasizes) to surrounding organs and tissues.

cardiac—pertaining to the heart.

cardiovascular system [*kar-dee-oh-vass'-kew-lur*]—the heart, arteries, and veins; the circulatory system.

carpal joint [*kar'-pul*]—the joint between the short pastern bone and the coffin bone.

carpitis—see **popped knee**

carriage—a four-wheeled driving vehicle that carries passengers comfortably.

carriage lining (also "carriage trim")—the upholstery inside a carriage.

carrier—1) an individual that carries a recessive gene for a trait, without exhibiting that trait; 2) (also "vector") the organism, animal, or insect that transmits a disease, without being affected by that disease.

cart (also "roadster" "road cart" "jog cart" "pleasure cart")—a 2-wheeled driving vehicle for racing and/or pleasure driving.

cartilage—a tough, fibrous, whitish connective tissue attached to the bones.

Caslick's operation—a procedure where a section of the vulval lips are stitched together to prevent air and contaminants from entering the reproductive tract; usually performed on mares that have had trouble carrying a foal to term.

cast—1) term for when a horse that rolls in its stall becomes wedged against a wall so that it cannot get up without help; 2) in foxhunting, when the hounds spread out to pick up the scent.

castration (also "gelding")—removal of the testicles.

cataract—opacity or lack of transparency in the lens of the eye.

catch rope—in roping, the rope that is thrown to catch the animal.

catheter—a tube used for withdrawing or introducing fluids from or into a body cavity.

caudal—toward the tail.

causative—the situation or condition that is responsible for a problem.

caustic—having the capacity to burn tissues or skin.

cauterize—to destroy dead or unwanted tissue to prevent the spread of infection.

cavaletti [*kav-uh-leh'-tee*] (also "trotting poles" "cross rails")—a series of poles laid out 4 to 4 1/2 feet apart; they are used to make the horse trot more steadily, to encourage it to lengthen its stride, and pick up the feet; this improves balance, and strengthens muscles.

cavesson [*kav'-eh-sahn*]—a simple noseband with two straps that buckle together on the side and pass behind the head.

"cavvy"—see **remuda**

cayuse [*kye'-yous*]—1) an Indian horse or pony; 2) slang for a western horse.

cellular—consisting of cells.

central nervous system—brain, spinal cord, cranial nerves, and spinal nerves.

certification—see **accreditation**

cervical—pertaining to the neck.

cervical os—opening of the cervix of the uterus.

cervicitis—inflammation of the cervix.

cervix—the muscular structure separating the opening of the uterus from the vagina.

cesarean section—a surgical procedure where a foal is delivered through an abdominal incision in the mare.

chaff—meadow hay or green straw used for feed.

chain shank—used for restraint in stallions and high-strung horses; consists of a chain 12" to 18" long, having flattened links, that is either attached to the halter and then placed over the horse's nose or under the lower jaw, or run underneath the upper lip inside the mouth.

champion—in showing, the first place winner in a class made up of all the first place winners in that division.

chaps—leather leggings used for protection, warmth, and to provide a secure seat in the saddle; used in western style riding.

Charley (also "Charles" "Charles James" "Uncle Remus" "Reynard")—in foxhunting, a common name for the fox.

chase—see **steeplechase**

check—1) a strap that keeps the horse's head up; 2) in foxhunting, a halt after the hounds lose the scent; 3) in racing, slowing a horse because other horses are in the way.

check and release (also "give and take")—using the reins to steady the horse by slight pulling and then releasing.

check apparatus—a system of muscles that aid in keeping the forelimbs in extension.

check rein (also "bearing rein")—the outside rein used to "check" the horse's speed.

cheekpiece (also "cheekstrap")—the strap on the bridle that attaches to the cheek of the bit.

cheeks (also "shanks")—the arms of the bit; these can be of various lengths for more or less leverage.

chestnut—1) (also "night eyes") a horny growth on the inner side of a horse's legs, just above the knee in front and below the hock in back; can be used for positive identification of a horse; 2) (also "sorrel") a haircoat with a reddish-brown color; mane and tail are the same color; **flaxen c.** is accompanied by light color mane and tail; **liver c.** is body coat where brown is predominant hair color.

chime—in hunting, when the hounds bay in unison when they are on the scent of the fox.

chiropractic—treating disease and/or pain by the manipulation of joints and bones to restore proper nerve function.

choke—(*n*) describes an obstruction of the breathing passages or esophagus.

chromosomes—bodies within the cell nucleus that are composed of DNA and carry genetic information.

chronic—continuous, long term.

Chronic Obstructive Pulmonary Disease—see **heaves**

chukka [*chu´-kuh*]—in polo, a period of play lasting about 8 minutes.

cinch (also "cincha")—the girth strap on a western saddle; holds the saddle in place.

circle—in jumping, the term for a fault given when the horse crosses any track made before it jumped the last obstacle.

claiming—in racing, when a person purchases, for a predetermined price, a horse that is entered in a race; ownership takes effect after the race begins, however the former owner is entitled to the winnings of that race.

class—an event within a division at a horse show; i.e., ladies class in hunter.

classic—1) in racing, any one of the five chief English flat races for 3-year olds; the Derby, the Oaks, the St. Leger, the 1,000 Guineas, and the 2,000 Guineas; 2) a race or show of traditional importance.

clear round—in show jumping or cross country, a round completed without faults.

cleft palate—a deviated septum; characterized by an opening in the soft palate that allows food and fluid to move from the mouth cavity into the nasal passages.

click—see **nick**

clinic—an educational meeting to provide information on some aspect of horse-related care or training.

clinical—direct treatment and observation.

closebreeding (*not in current use;* see **inbreeding**)—extreme inbreeding such as brother to sister, parent to offspring.

closed knees—when long bone growth is complete.

clover—a legume used for hay and pasture.

cloverleaf barrel—a western pattern for maneuvering the horse around three barrels in the correct order, as fast as possible.

cloverleaf pattern—a test pattern where each "leaf" of the pattern must be executed in a particular order.

club foot—a deformity caused by either improper trimming, excessive chipping of the hoof wall at the toe, or inherited short, steep pasterns; a club foot has an axis of 60 degrees or more.

clubhouse turn—in racing, generally the first turn after the finish line.

coach housing (also "pad cloth")—in driving, the cloth or leather piece that is used under the pad or saddle on harness.

cob—a short-legged horse, maximum height 15.1 hh, with bone and substance of a heavy weight hunter; capable of carrying substantial weight; a type, not a breed.

coffin bone—the most important bone in the horse's foot, directly under the hoof wall, providing a surface for attachment of blood vessels and nerves and as a point of attachment for the deep flexor and main extensor tendons.

coffin joint—within the hoof, the joint between the short pastern bone and the coffin bone, and including the navicular bone.

Coggins test—a test for the virus causing Equine Infectious Anemia.

coitus [*koh´-ih-tus*]—see **copulation**

cold-blood—term for heavy draft and work horses; type developed in the northern regions and were characterized by large, strong, calm-tempered animals.

cold hunting—in foxhunting, when the scent of the fox has grown so old that the hounds have difficulty picking it up.

cold line—in hunting, a stale or old, faint scent.

"cold mouth"—term referring to a horse that does not salivate when bitted up.

collar—on harness, a leather collar that fits over the horse's head, and rests on the shoulders.

colic—sharp abdominal pain, often a symptom of gas pain of abdominal origin or an obstruction created by food or feces; can lead to a twisted bowel and death.

colicky—having the symptoms of colic.

collateral relatives—sharing common ancestors; i.e., cousins.

collection—the condition of engaging the hindquarters, positioning the head just in front of the vertical, and moving forward in a free, but controlled manner.

colon—the large intestine.

colors—1) in foxhunting, the colors that distinguish the various hunts from each other; 2) in racing-see **silks**; 3) approved coat colors for registration of horses

colostrum [*koh-lahs´-trum*]—the first milk given by a mammal. Mare's colostrum contains important antibodies which are absorbed by the foal within 24-36 hours after-birth.

colt—a young ungelded male horse under 4 years old.

comatose [*koh´-mah-tohss*]—in a state of coma; unconscious.

combination obstacle—in show jumping, two or more jumps that are numbered and are considered and judged as one obstacle.

Combined Immunodeficiency Disease (CID)—predominantly found in Arabian foals, this inherited deficiency of the infection-fighting lymphocytes is always fatal.

combined training competition—a comprehensive test for horse and rider, consisting of three phases: dressage, cross-country, and show jumping.

"come-along" (see also **butt rope**)—a rope harness used for teaching foals to lead.

command—see **cue** and **verbals**

compensatory growth—accelerated growth rate experienced by youngstock when given adequate nutrition after being undernourished.

competitive ride—an overland ride completed in a specified amount of time.

complete ration—feed (usually in pellet form) that contains all the nutrients required by the horse.

composition—make-up.

compromise—to make weak or vulnerable.

concave—hollow and curved.

conceive (also "settle")—become pregnant.

concentrates—grain or pelleted feed.

conception—becoming pregnant.

concussion—shock from impact.

Condition Book—in racing, the book which lists which races are available and the conditions, such as age, sex, weight, distance, etc.; maintained by the Racing Secretary.

conditioning—physical exercise and training of a horse to bring it to its full athletic potential for a particular use.

condom—a rubber bag fitted to the stallion's penis for collecting semen.

conformation—structure of the horse's body.

conformation class—see **halter class**

congenital—a condition present at birth; these defects may or may not be hereditary.

conjunctiva [*kon-junk-tye´-vuh*]—the lining membrane of the eyelid that protects the exposed sclerae (whites).

connective tissue—fibrous tissue that binds and supports body structures.

consign—put a horse up for auction or sale by paying a nonrefundable fee.

contact—the connection, through the reins, between the rider's hands and the horse's mouth.

contagious—able to be passed from one individual to another.

Contagious Equine Metritis (CEM)—a highly contagious disease in mares that causes inflammation of the cervical, uterine, and vaginal membranes.

Continental bridle—a show bridle crafted in two-tone or tone-on-tone leather.

Continental browband—a browband decorated in a pattern of colored squares.

contracted heels—an abnormally low heel, sunken frog, the parallel hoof bars resulting in lameness; can be inherited or caused by poor shoeing.

contracted tendons—the condition in which a foal's deep flexor tendons are shorter than normal, preventing it from flexing the fetlock joint normally; the foal stands with pasterns upright and bears its weight on the toe, with heels not touching the ground; foals are either born with this condition or develop it very soon after birth.

convulsions—a violent, involuntary contraction or spasm of the muscles.

Convulsive Foal Syndrome (CFS) (also "barker foal" or "dummy foal")—a condition characterized by convulsions, blindness, weakness, and a barking noise; it is thought to be caused by lack of oxygen during birth.

cooler—a heavy blanket used on a horse after a workout.

"cooling out"—the process of allowing a horse's body temperature to return to normal so that it does not get chilled or become sick.

coon foot—conformation in which the pastern is excessively long, with more slope than the anterior surface of the hoof wall.

coop—in jumping, a fence consisting of two panels attached at the top back to back, with the appearance of a triangle.

coprophagy [*ka-prah´-fuh-gee*]—ingestion of manure; eating feces.

copulation—the act of mating; sexual intercourse.

corn—a bruise of the sole at the angle between the heel and the wall of the hoof.

coronary band—the growth and nutritional source for the hoofwall; located around the top of the hoof wall.

coronary cushion—the elastic portion of the coronary band in the hoof.

coronet marking—white ring around the coronet of the hoof.

Corpus luteum—a yellow body in the ovary that secretes progesterone, an important reproductive hormone.

corral—a pen for animals, usually made of wood.

corticosteroid—any hormone secreted by the adrenal cortex, or a compound derived from these, or synthetic compounds with similar structures.

Corynebacterium equi [*kor-nee-bak-teer´-ee-um ee´-kwye*]—bacteria found in the soil; cause of foal pneumonia.

counter-canter—in showing, at the judge's request, to go clockwise around the ring, but canter on the left lead.

counter-irritant—a topical analgesic that produces severe irritation to the skin and promotes a large increase of blood flow to the area.

couple—in hunting, two hounds.

coupling—the section between the point of the hip and the last rib.

Courbette [*koor-bett´*]—an "air above the ground," from the Spanish Riding School, in which the horse rears to almost upright, then leaps forward on its hind legs several times.

course—1) a race course; 2) in show jumping and cross-country, a circuit of obstacles to be jumped in a certain order within a certain time limit; 3) in hunting, for hounds to hunt by sight rather than by scent.

course designer—one who designs and supervises the construction of jumps and lay-out of a jumping or eventing course.

covered—bred, mated.

covert [*cuh´-ver*]—in hunting, a thicket or small area of woods.

cow hocks—conformation fault combining base-wide and hocks too close together.

cow horse—a horse trained for herding cattle.

cow kick—a kick forward or out to the side, rather than straight back.

cowboy/cowgirl—one who tends and herds cattle.

cranium—the skeleton of the head, or skull.

cradle—see **bib**

creep feeder—a device that allows a foal to eat, but keeps the dam or other pasturemates from feeding.

cremello—a horse with pink skin, blue eyes, and ivory-colored hair.

cribbing (also "windsucking" "stump sucking")—a vice usually acquired due to boredom, but becomes a habit; the horse grabs the edge of the stall door or fence, pulls back and gulps air.

cribbing strap—device used on the horse's neck that prevents air swallowing.

crooked (also "not straight")—during movement, the hindquarters swing to the inside, or when the horse stops, the hindquarters are to one side.

crop 1) (also "bat")—a riding aid consisting of a short stiff stick, measuring 18-24 inches long, and having a flat popper on the end that is meant to make a loud noise; 2) the foals of an individual sire in a year.

cropper (also "crumpler" "crowner")—a bad fall.

crossbred—(*n*) the offspring of two different breeds.

crossbreeding—(*v*) mating horses of two different breeds.

crossbuck—see **sawbuck**

cross-cantering—see **cross-firing**

cross-firing (also "disunited" "cross cantering")—1) a form of "interference"; a gait abnormality in which the inside of the toe or inside wall of hind foot strikes the inner quarter of the opposite forefoot; 2) cantering behind on opposite leads.

cross rail—1) in jumping, a fence that looks like a flattened "X" with a center about 6 inches high; 2) in ground work, rails laid out on the ground (see also **cavaletti**).

cross-tie—*(v)* to a tie horse from two sides, with ropes running from the wall to the halter on either side; *(n)* a rope with snaps at both ends, one of which is usually a panic-snap.

Croupade [*kroo-pahd´*]—an "air above the ground" in which the horse rears and jumps straight up, drawing the hind legs up toward the belly.

croup [*kroop*]—top of the rump.

croupier—see **crupper**

crow hop—small quick jumps where all four feet are off the ground.

crown—semi-circle marking above the front part of the hoof.

crown piece (also "head piece")—the bridle strap that runs across the crown of the horse's head.

crowner—see **cropper**

crude protein—total nitrogen content in feed.

crumpler—see **cropper**

crupper (also "croupier")—part of harness that goes around the tail and is then attached to the back strap to keep the saddle in proper position.

cryosurgery—the procedure in which a freezing process is used to remove something, such as a wart or lesion.

cryotherapy (also "icing")—treatment of disease or pain by lowering the body temperature, as with ice packs.

cryptorchidism [*kript-or´-kid-dizm*]—failure of one or both testicles to descend to the scrotum after birth; testes may be retained within the abdominal cavity or inguinal canal.

Cuboni test [*kew-boh´-nee*]—pregnancy test, done at 120 to 290 days' gestation, that detects estrogen in the mare's urine.

cue (also "command")—a signal given by the handler or rider.

culling (see also **artificial selection**)—the elimination of undesirable animals from a breeding herd.

culture—a diagnostic test in which microorganisms taken from an individual are grown in a special medium under controlled conditions.

curb—thickening of the ligament that runs along the back of the hock; caused by strain.

curb bit—bit used with a snaffle bit in a double bridle; consists of two cheekpieces and a mouthpiece with a central port; the most common leverage type bit.

curb chain or strap—a metal chain fitted to a curb or Pelham bit; it lies in the curb groove of the horse's jaw, providing leverage.

curb groove—the groove in front of the lower jawbones, just behind the horse's chin.

curettage [*cure-eh-tahzh´*]—scraping the interior of a cavity, usually the uterus.

curry—*(v)* the act of combing or brushing a horse's hair coat.

currycomb—grooming equipment used to remove dirt and scurf from a horse's coat; has a flat back with the front containing several rows of rubber or metal teeth.

cut—1) *(v)* to separate out cattle from the herd; 2) see **geld**

cut and set—a practice where the tail is surgically cut and then set to heal in a very upright position; done only on gaited Saddle Horses, Hackney Ponies, and Tennessee Walking Horses.

cut down—injuries a horse sustains from being struck by another horse's shoes, or by its own shoes due to faulty stride.

"cut out under the knees"—a condition in which the bone and tendons are too small under the knees.

cutaneous [*kew-tay´-nee-us*]—pertaining to the skin.

cutter—term for a horse used for cutting cattle or the cowboy who cuts cattle.

cutting horse—a specially-trained horse used for separating cattle from a herd.

cyanosis [*sigh-an-oh´-sis*]—purple coloring of mucous membranes resulting from reduced blood oxygenation.

cycling (also "short cycle")—artificially stimulating a mare's heat cycle in order to adjust it.

cyst—any closed cavity, especially one containing fluid.

cystic—having cysts.

cytology—having to do with cells and their structure and pathology.

 # D

DMSO—*dimethylsulfoxide;* a liquid that diffuses rapidly through the skin and is used as a carrying agent or solvent, especially for anti-inflammatory agents; it can be dangerous, since it will carry any agent, including poisons.

DNA—*deoxyribonucleic acid;* the material that makes up chromosomes and carries genetic information for every cell.

D.V.M.—Doctor of Veterinary Medicine.

daily double (also "double" "late double")—in racing, backing two horses to win in two consecutive races.

dally—in roping, when a roper wraps the rope around the saddle horn one or more times to secure the rope.

dally roping—in team roping, when the header catches the steer's horns, he dallies his rope around the saddle horn and moves the steer off so that the heeler can rope the feet and dally his rope to the saddle horn to stop the steer.

dam—the mother of a horse.

dandy brush (also "mud brush")—long-bristled brush for removing the surface dirt or mud.

dappled—a haircoat having spots of contrasting colors.

dark horse—in racing, an unknown horse.

day coat—in saddleseat attire, a long tailored riding jacket.

dead heat—in racing, a tie for any of the first three places.

debilitation—weakness.

debridement [*day-breed'-munt*]—the surgical removal of foreign matter or diseased tissue in a wound or organ.

debris [*day-bree'*]—any foreign matter found in a body cavity or wound

declaration—an owner or trainer's statement in writing that a horse will compete in a particular competition.

defecation—excretion of waste matter from the bowels.

deficient—lacking.

degenerative—of a deteriorating nature, breaking down.

degenerative joint disease—arthritis that causes bone to replace the cartilage of a joint; this reduces the joint's range of motion.

dehydration—abnormal depletion of body fluids; loss of water.

dentition [*den-tih'-shun*]—1) development or cutting of teeth; 2) dental structure.

depressive—having the ability to depress.

depth perception—the ability to see objects in perspective.

Dermatophilosis [*der-ma-tow-fill-oh'-sus*]—clinical name for a skin condition commonly known as "rain rot," "pasture rot," or "rain scald."

Dermatophilus congolensis [*der-ma-tow-fyl'-us kong-go-len'-sus*]—bacteria which cause "rain rot," etc.

dermatophyte [*der-ma'-tow-fyte*]—the bacteria that causes "ringworm."

Dermatophytosis [*der-ma-tow-fy-tow'-sus*]—clinical name for skin condition commonly known as "ringworm."

dermoid [*der'-moyd*]—a growth that resembles skin.

deviation—anything other than normal or standard.

deworming—process of administering drugs that kill internal parasites.

diagonal—in opposite corners; the opposite legs that form a pair when the horse is moving; i.e., the right foreleg and left hindleg are diagonal.

diaphragm [*dy´-uh-fram*]—the muscle/membrane wall between the abdominal and thoracic cavities.

diathermy—treatment of disease or pain by the application of heat.

diestrus [*dy-ess´-truss*]—the period of a mare's estrous cycle when she will not accept a stallion.

differential diagnosis—making a diagnosis based on the comparison of symptoms from several possible diseases.

digestible energy—the amount of total energy in feed that can be digested and used.

digit—on a horse, the portion of leg below the fetlock.

digital cushion—area beneath the coffin bone that separates it from the frog and acts as a shock absorber.

dilation—being expanded or wider.

direct pressure—control by using a bit that pulls directly backward or sideways on the mouth or nose.

direct rein (also "plow rein" "opening rein")—opening the rein in the direction that the rider wants the horse to move.

dirt track—in racing, a track with a surface made of sand and soil.

dished sole—increased concavity of the sole of the hoof.

dismount—1) to get down from the saddle; 2) when a stallion gets off the mare after breeding.

dismount sample—the small amount of semen that trickles out of the penis after the stallion has bred a mare and dismounted.

disposition—see **temperament**

disproportionate—not in proportion.

distaff—in racing, a female horse.

distal—remote or out away from the point of attachment.

distal spots—see **ermine spots**

distemper—see **strangles**

distention—inflated or expanded with gas or solid matter.

disunited—see **cross-firing**

diuretic [*dy-yur-reh´-tik*]—substance that increases urine secretion.

dividend (also "pay-off")—in racing, the amount paid out to the backers of a winning or placing horse.

dock—the attachment of the tail.

dog fox—a male fox.

dog hound—a male hound.

dominant—1) in genetics, a term for describing an allele that overrides another allele; 2) overpowering or overriding.

donor mare—the mare that produces and contributes an embryo for embryo transfer procedure.

dope—*(v)* to illegally administer drugs to a horse to either improve or hinder its performance.

Doppler Principle—an apparent change in wave frequency produced by motion of the source toward or away from the stationary observer, or by motion of the observer toward or away from the stationary source.

dorsal—pertaining to the back, or toward the back.

dorsal stripe—a dark line running down the center of the back on dun horses.

double— 1) in show jumping, a combination obstacle consisting of two jumps; 2) in foxhunting, a series of short sharp notes blown on the horn to signal that the fox is on foot; 3) in racing (see **daily double**)

double bridle—a bridle with two bits-a curb and a snaffle-attached by two cheekpieces; they may be operated independently of each other.

draft horse (also "draught horse")—a large, very strong horse used for work on the farm or in the woods.

drag—1) in hunting, an artificial scent made by infusing a piece of sacking with fox droppings or aniseed, then dragging it over the ground; 2) in driving, a training device consisting of a board or light-weight rail "hooked" to the harness; used to accustom the horse to pulling weight.

draghound—a hound trained to follow a drag.

draghunt—a hunt using a drag.

draught horse—see **draft horse**

dress livery—in driving, the formal working uniform of the groom or coachman.

dress points—in driving attire, accessories including gloves, boots, tie, hankey, and hat.

dressage [*dreh-sahj´*]—training horses to perform movements with balance, suppleness, obedience, and brilliance.

dressage boot—a low-heeled English style riding boot that reaches to just below the knee.

dressage whip—see **training whip**

"drive-on" trot—a roadster driving gait that is the fastest trot.

driving apron (also "lap robe")—a square of material that covers the driver's lap and knees.

driving whip—a driving aid of approximately 4 to 5 feet, made of rawhide, and having silk lashes at the tip.

dropped—(*v*) slang term for delivery of a foal.

dropped sole (also "pumiced foot")—abnormal foot conformation where the sole has dropped below the weight bearing surface of the hoof wall, causing lameness.

"dropping the horse"—in jumping, releasing the horse just before the jump, which surprises it and throws off its rhythm.

drover—Australian horseman who herds cattle or sheep for long distances.

dry-joint—see **ankylosed**

duct—a tubular passage that conveys fluid.

ductus arteriosus [*duck´-tus ar-teer-ee-oh´-sus*]—a vessel in a fetus that connects the left pulmonary artery and the aorta; after birth and within the first two months, the vessel turns into a fibrous cord.

dummy foal—see **Convulsive Foal Syndrome**

dummy mare (also "phantom mare")—a padded structure that is mounted by the stallion while semen is being collected.

dun—hair coat of a sandy yellow, reddish, or light brown color, sometimes with darker legs and a dark stripe down the back (dorsal stripe); often with dark mane & tail.

Dutch collar—see **breastplate**

dwarfism—the genetic possibility of producing stunted, malformed, or deformed offspring.

dysfunction—impaired or abnormal state.

dystocia [*dis-tow´-shuh*]—difficult delivery or birth.

 # E

EEE—see **Equine encephalomyelitis**

EI—see **Equine Influenza**

EIA—see **Equine Infectious Anemia**

EVA—see **Equine Viral Arteritis**

"each way"—in racing, to back a horse to win and finish in the first three.

early embryonic death—death of the embryo before day 30 of gestation.

earth (also "lair")—in hunting, the den of a fox.

"easy keeper"—a horse that doesn't require much feed in order to stay fit.

edema—accumulation of fluid in the tissues or body cavities, causing swelling.

egg butt snaffle—a bit having snaffle rings with a non-pinching hinge.

ejaculate—(*v*) the discharge of semen during breeding.

ejaculation—emission of seminal fluid.

electrolyte solution—a salt and water solution that is used to replace those salts in the blood that are lost through excessive heat or stress.

elimination—removing a competitor from an event.

emaciate—to lose body flesh.

embryo—an organism during the earliest stages of development; in the horse, up to approximately 40 days of gestation.

embryo transfer—procedure that takes a developing embryo from its natural mother and implants it in the uterus of a host mother for the remainder of the gestation.

emphysema [*em-fih-see´-muh*]—see **heaves**

encapsulated—enclosed in a capsule or sheath.

encephalomalacia [*en-sef´-uh-low-muh-lay´-shuh*]—cerebral softening, usually a result of cutting off the blood supply.

endemic—native to a particular region.

endocrine [*en´-doe-kryn*]—referring to glands and structures that secrete hormones into blood or lymph.

endometritis [*en-doe-meh-try´-tus*]—inflammation of the mucous membrane of the uterus.

endometrium [*en-doe-mee´-tree-um*]—the lining of the uterine wall.

endoscope—an instrument used to examine hollow internal organs or body cavities; sometimes attached to a videocamera.

endoscopic—pertaining to examination of the inside of a hollow body cavity.

endurance ride—a race to be completed in the shortest time and with horses in the best condition.

endurance saddle—a lightweight saddle composed of the best features of English and western saddlery; designed to adapt to the horse's action.

engaged—1) in racing, a horse that is entered in a particular race; 2) another term for "engaging the hocks."

engagement or "engaging the hocks"—a condition where the hind legs are well under the body and the haunches are lowered through flexion of the stifle and hocks.

enlarged knee—see **popped knee**

enteritis [*en-tur-rye´-tus*]—inflammation of the intestinal lining.

enterolith—a stone that forms around a foreign object in the horse's intestine; can eventually lead to colic and death.

entry—term for a horse and/or exhibitor that will compete in a class.

entry book—see **premium book**

environment—all the external conditions that affect and influence an individual.

enzyme—a protein capable of accerlerating or producing change in another substance without itself being changed.

epidural anesthesia [*eh-pih-dur´-ul*]—a spinal anesthesia.

epinephrine [*eh-pih-neh´-frin*]—adrenal gland hormone that raises blood pressure.

epiphyseal plate [*ee-pih´-fih-seel*]—the growth plate between the long bones of the legs.

epiphysis [*ee-pih´-fih-sus*]—the end of a long bone.

epiphysitis [*ee-pih-fih-sye´-tus*] (also "osteochondritis" "osteochondrosis")—swelling or inflammation of the epiphyseal, or growth, plate.

episiotomy [*ee-pee-see-ah´-tih-mee*]—incision of the sutured vulva.

epistaxis [*eh-pih-stack´-sis*]—bleeding from the nose.

equestrian—1) pertaining to horsemanship or horsemen; 2) a rider.

equestrienne—a female involved in horsemanship or riding.

equine [*ee´-kwine*]—1) family of Equidae, including horses, asses, and zebras; 2) a horse; of or pertaining to horses.

Equine Encephalomyelitis [*en-sef´-uh-low-my-eh-lye´-tis*] (also "sleeping sickness")—an acute viral disease of the horse causing inflammation of the brain and spinal cord; carried by migrating birds and transmitted by biting flies and mosquitos; there are three strains: (EEE) Eastern Equine E., (WEE) Western Equine E., and (VEE) Venezuelan Equine E.

Equine Infectious Anemia (also "Swamp Fever")—a viral infection that is spread by biting flies and the improper use of hypodermic needles; it causes edema, weight loss, fever, and anemia.

Equine Influenza (EI)—an acute, infectious, contagious viral disease, characterized by inflammation of the respiratory tract, fever, and muscular pain.

Equine Viral Arteritis (EVA)—highly contagious disease in horses that causes swelling of the legs and, in stallions, swelling of the scrotum; causes abortion in mares.

equitation [*eh-kwih-tay´-shun*]—the art of riding, with concentration on perfecting all aspects of horsemanship form and ability.

equus [*eh´-kwus*]—zoological classification that includes horses, zebras, and asses.

erectile tissue—tissue having spaces that become engorged with blood, thus becoming firm.

erection—the blood engorgement of the penis that causes it to become rigid.

ergot [*er´-got*]—1) horny growth at the back of the fetlock joint; 2) a fungus of rye that, upon ingestion, causes uterine contractions and abortion.

ermine spots (also "distal spots")—black or colored spots on the white marking near the coronary band.

erratic—not consistent or regular.

erythrocyte [*air-rith´-row-site*]—red blood cell.

esophageal [*ee-sah-fah-jeel´*]—pertaining to the esophagus.

estradiol [*ehs-trah-dye´-all*]—the female sex hormone.

estrogen—a substance produced by the ovary, placenta, and testes.

estrous cycle—the complete reproductive cycle of the mare.

estrus (also "in heat" "in season" "horsing")—the time during a mare's cycle when she is receptive to a stallion.

eugenics [*you-jen´-iks*]—the study of the conditions that could improve the quality of future generations in a breeding program.

eumelanin—the black or brown form of melanin pigment granules.

euthanize [*you´-than-eyes*] (also "put down")—to kill or put an animal to sleep for humane reasons.

"evens" (also "even money")—in racing, betting odds given on a horse when the bettor can win the same amount as his stake.

event horse—one that competes or is trained to compete in a combined training competition.

evert—extrude.

ewe neck (also "upside-down neck")—having a topline concave at the neck.

exacerbated [*ex-sass´-ser-bay-ted*]—intensified, made worse.

exacta (also "perfecta") [*"exactor" in Canada*]—wagering where the bettor selects the first and second place winners in exact order.

exercise rider—in racing, a rider who is licensed to exercise a racehorse during its morning training session.

exhibitor (also "handler")—in showing, the person riding, driving, or presenting the horse.

extended—1) having the legs out in a straight line; 2) in racing, running at top speed.

extension—movement that brings a limb into a straight line; lengthening of stride.

extrauterine—outside of the uterus.

exudate [*ex´-oo-date*]—any fluid that is formed as a result of an injury or infection.

 F

FPT—see failure of passive transfer

FSH—see Follicle Stimulating Hormone

face—1) in team roping, when both partners make their catch and the horses are facing the steer; the run is complete and time is called; 2) the front of the horse's head.

face drop—decoration that hangs from the bridle browband on harness.

failure of passive transfer (also "FPT")—a condition in which the foal does not receive or utilize the antibodies from the mare's colostrum.

fallopian tube [*fah-low´-pee-an*]—the tube from the ovary to the fallopian attachment at the end of the uterine horn; it carries the egg to the uterus.

false martingale—see **breastplate**

"fancied"—see **favorite**

far side—see **off side**

farrier [*fair´-ee-er*] (also "blacksmith" "horseshoer" "shoer" "plater")—a person who trims hooves, performs routine or corrective maintenance on feet, and shoes horses.

fast track—in racing, term for a track that is even, dry, and resilient.

fault—(*n*) weak points in conformation; in show-jumping, scoring unit used to record a knockdown, refusal or other offense by a competitor.

favorite (also "fancied")—in racing, the term for a horse that is likely to win a particular race; the horse having the shortest odds offered against it.

feathers—the long hairs that grow just above and cover the fetlocks.

febrile [*feh´-bryl*]—feverish.

feces—manure.

fee—1) in showing, the money paid for each class entry; 2) (also "jockey fee") in racing, the money paid to a jockey for a race; 3) the money paid to nominate, enter, or start a horse in a stakes race.

feed bag—a canvas bag that attaches to the horse's bridle, allowing it to eat when traveling or working away from home.

fence (also "jump" "rail")—1) in jumping, term for a jump that is constructed to look like a fence; (see also **brush box, coop, oxer, panel, Texas gate, treble triple bar, wall fence**); 2) in racing, the racetrack side barriers; 3) barrier around a pasture/paddock.

fenders (also "rosadero")—leather panels that cover the stirrup leathers on a western saddle.

feral—not domesticated.

fertile—reproductively healthy.

fertility—the ability to reproduce.

fertilization—when sperm and egg join together.

fescue—a grass that has been proven to cause abortion in mares.

fetal—having to do with a fetus.

fetlock—the tuft of hair at the back of the ankle.

fetlock joint—the ankle joint.

fetotomy [*fee-tah´-tuh-mee*]—a surgical procedure where a dead fetus is cut up to facilitate removal from the mare.

fetus—an unborn organism during the later stages of growth and development.

fiador—an optional rope throatlatch on a hackamore bridle.

fibrin—protein in the blood that aids in clotting.

fibrosis—abnormal increase in fibrous connective tissue.

fibroplastic—having the appearance of scar tissue or proud flesh.

field—(*n*) 1) in hunting, the mounted followers of a hunt; 2) in racing, all the horses running or all the horses not individually favored in betting.

field boot—a low-heeled English style boot reaching to just below the knee and having laces up the front.

fieldmaster—in hunting, the individual designated to control the field.

figure-8—an "8"-shaped riding pattern used for training and showing horses.

figure-8 noseband (also "Grackle")—composed of two straps that criss-cross the nose and buckle under the chin.

filly—a young female horse under two years of age.

fines—dust particles in grain.

finish—1) when the mounted horse passes the winning post; 2) term that describes putting the polish or finishing touches on training; i.e., a "finished horse."

finishing brush—a brush with very soft, flexible bristles used on face and ears or to put the final touch on a show coat.

fistula [*fish´-chew-lah*]—a fluid-draining tract that goes deep into tissues.

fistulous withers—infection of the withers that extends down into the shoulder muscles; usually caused by neglect of saddle sores.

fittings (also "hardware")—metal parts on leather tack that keep all the pieces together and functional.

fixture—see **appointment card**

flagging—*(v)* the rhythmic waving of a stallion's tail as he ejaculates.

flagellum [*flah-jel´-um*]—the tail of the spermatozoa, used for propulsion.

flake—a unit of measure for feeding hay, usually about 4-5 pounds.

flank—the area between the ribs and the hip.

flapper—in racing, a horse that runs at an unauthorized meeting.

flapping—an unofficial race not held under the rules of racing.

flares—hoof deformities where the hoof wall spreads outwards and curves up.

flash cavesson—see **cavesson**

flat feet—abnormal conformation of the hoof in which there is no concavity of the sole.

flat jumping saddle—see **saddle, English; close-contact**

flat racing—a competition in which there are no obstacles to jump.

flat strides—little or no suspension in the sequence.

flat walk—a 4-beat gait; it is the natural gait of Tennessee Walking Horses.

flat work—riding or schooling a horse on flat ground, rather than jumping.

fleck—small patch of white hair.

Flehmen response [*flay´-man*]—the horse's reaction to novel or pleasurable smells; characterized by curling back the upper lip and inhaling deeply.

flexion—bending; **direct f.**—flexion from the hind legs to the head; **lateral f.**—bending the spine so that the hind feet follow in the tracks of the front feet around a curve, with the neck bent in the same curve as the backbone.

flexor tendon—the tendon that runs from the head of the cannon bone, under the navicular bone, and attaches to the coffin bone.

float—*(v)* to remove the sharp edges from a horse's teeth.

flora—the normal, beneficial bacteria count of a body part.

flower—a star face marking that looks like a flower.

fly back—*(v)* when a horse suddenly pulls back violently, usually breaking the halter or tie rope.

fly whisk—a riding aid consisting of a stick with long horsehair at the tip.

flying change—changing leads at the canter or lope without breaking stride.

foal—*(n)* a baby horse; *(v)* to deliver a foal.

foal heat (also "nine-day heat")—the first heat after foaling.

foal watch—common term for around-the-clock observation of a mare that is about ready to deliver.

foaling—birthing or delivery of a baby horse.

foaling slip (also "Dutch slip")—a light leather or web halter for foals.

Follicle Stimulating Hormone (FSH)—the female hormone that stimulates the production of a follicle in the ovary.

follicle—the cell that encases and nourishes the egg as it develops within the ovary.

follicular stage—the portion of the mare's cycle during which the follicle is forming, between proestrus and estrus.

footing—1) the material used on the floor of an arena, ring, or track; 2) the ground or area on which a horse works; 3) contact with the ground, as in "get his footing."

forage—food for domestic animals, fodder.

foramen ovale [*for-ah´-men oh-vol´-ee*]—an opening in the fetal heart which closes shortly after birth.

foregirth—a girth used on a horse with low withers.

forehand—the term used to describe the head, neck, withers, shoulders and forelegs of the horse collectively.

forelock—the long locks of hair that grow from between the ears and hang down over the forehead.

forging—a form of "interference"; the term used to describe the toe of the hind foot striking the toe of the front foot while the horse is in motion.

form—in racing, the past performance of a horse.

forward seat (also "hunt seat")—English-style riding where the rider keeps his weight over the horse's withers; also used in jumping.

founder—see **laminitis**

founder rings—grooves in the wall of the hoof that are caused by a disturbance of the growth rate; a result of laminitis (founder).

four-in-hand—in driving, a hitch or team of four horses.

fox trot—a slow, short, broken trot usually accompanied by nodding of the head with the foreward movement.

foxhunting—the sport of hunting the fox in its natural state using a pack of hounds and people on horses or on foot.

fracture—any broken bone or bony part of the skeleton; **comminuted f.**-one with more than two fragments; **compound f.**-one where the bone breaks through the skin; **condylar f.**-one in the lower end of a long bone such as cannon or humerus; **simple f.**-one that follows a single line and does not penetrate the skin; **stress f.**-one that results from excessive stress on the bone from athletic or performance training and use.

freeze brand—see **freeze mark**

free-lance trainer—one who works as a self-employed trainer, rather than as an employee of a facility; an independent contractor.

freeze mark (also "freeze brand")—an identification scar left by a cold marking instrument that causes the hair to grow in white.

French saddle—see **saddle, English; close-contact**

fresh line—in hunting, the term for a fresh scent.

Friedman test—a pregnancy test for mares.

frog—the triangular horny pad in the sole of a horse's foot that is the foot's circulatory mechanism.

full-brother, sister—horses that are produced by the same sire and dam.

full cry—in hunting, when all the hounds vocalize while on the scent.

full gallop—see **gallop**

full mouth—referring to a horse's mouth that has grown all its teeth.

full term—being fully mature at birth.

fungus—a plant-like organism that feeds on organic matter.

furlong (also "panel")—in racing, one-eighth of a mile, 220 yards, 660 feet.

furniture—see **mountings**

futurity—an incentive program for breeders wherein their foals are nominated and kept eligible by a series of fees paid at specific times; these horses are then eligible to compete in selected futurity classes or races.

fuzztail running—the act of herding and catching wild horses.

 # G

GRH—see **Gonadatropin Releasing Hormone**

gad—see **spur**

gag bridle—a severe bridle on which the cheekpieces are made of rounded leather and pass through the holes at the top and bottom of the bit rings, then attach directly to the reins.

gait—any of various foot movements of a horse, such as gallop, trot, canter.

gaited horse—a horse trained to perform any one of the artificial gaits known as pace, slow gait, and rack in addition to the three natural gaits (walk, trot, canter); usually only seen with Saddlebreds or Tennessee Walking Horses; **easy-gaited h.**-Tennessee Walking Horse, Missouri Foxtrotter, Paso Fino, and Peruvian Paso.

gaiter boot—see **jodhpur boot**

gall—a sore place that is usually caused by badly fitting tack.

gallop (also "run")—the canter speeded up, only with four beats instead of three and a longer suspension; a horse's fastest gait.

galloping boot—see **boot**

gamete—a germ cell: sperm or egg (ovum).

gangrene—death of tissue from lack of blood supply.

gaskin—the muscle between the hock and the stifle.

gastritis—inflammation of the stomach.

gastrointestinal—relating to the stomach and intestines.

gate—1) in jumping, a fence made of white planks or pickets between two side poles; 2) term for the entrance to a show ring or arena.

geld (also "cut" "alter")—to castrate

gelding—1) (n) a castrated male horse; 2) (v) the act of castrating a male horse.

gene—the determiner of hereditary traits; a segment of a DNA molecule.

genetic pool—all of the genes of a given population.

genetics—dealing with heredity or variation in similar or related animals and plants.

genitalia [jen-ih-tail'-yuh]—the genitals.

genitals—the reproductive organs.

genotype—the gene types that a horse inherits from both parents.

gentleman—in showing, a male adult exhibitor.

gentleman jockey—in steeplechase, an amateur rider.

gestation [jes-tay'-shun]—the growth and development period of the fetus inside the womb; in the horse, it is approximately 336 days (11 months).

get—the offspring or progeny of a stallion.

"get the gate"—in showing, 1) to be dismissed or excused from a class; 2) to not win a ribbon.

"getting ahead"—in jumping, the rider tries to leap into the jumping position just as the horse jumps, upsetting the horse's balance.

"getting in the horse's mouth"—exerting too much hand-pressure on the bit.

"getting left behind"—in jumping, the rider falls behind the horse's balance, coming down hard on the saddle and losing balance.

gig—an open 2-wheeled light driving vehicle, drawn by one horse.

"girl"—see **groom**

gingered tail—the application of an irritating substance, such as ginger, to the tender tissue around the anus; this causes the horse to hold the tail very high; considered a desirable effect in some show breeds.

girth—1) the circumference of the horse just behind the withers around the deepest part of the body; 2) a band of leather, webbing, or nylon that passes under the belly of the horse to secure the saddle or harness saddle.

girth mark—a mark behind the foreleg.

"give and take"—see **check and release**

gland—any secreting organ.

glandular—affected by or caused by glands

goat knees—see **over at the knee**

"going"—the condition of a race track or other ground over which a horse travels; as in, *soft going, good going*, etc.

"going out"—term used to describe the time when a mare becomes non-receptive to the stallion.

"going to cover"—in hunting, going to the meeting place of the hunt.

"golden slippers"—soft protective pads that cover a foal's hooves at birth; these keep the hooves from tearing the birth canal tissues during delivery.

gonads—sex organs; testes and ovaries.

Gonadatropin Releasing Hormone [*goh-nad´-uh-trow´-pin*]—the hormone that travels to the ovaries and stimulates the Follicle Stimulating Hormone.

"gone to ground"—in hunting, when the fox takes refuge in a drain or earth.

gonitis—inflammation of the stifle joint.

"good hands"—term to denote a rider that is gentle with the reins, while still cueing the horse correctly.

"good mouth"—a horse that produces saliva by mouthing the bit, thereby having a wet mouth; responding willingly to bit cues.

governess cart (also "tub")—a cart with a wicker body that can carry 4-6 passengers.

Graafian follicle [*gray´-fee-an*]—a mature ovarian follicle.

Grackle noseband—see **figure-8 noseband**

grade horse—a horse that is not registered.

grading—*(term not in current use)* breeding inferior female animals to better males to produce better offspring; not practiced consistently with horses.

granddam—second dam or "grandmother" of a horse.

grandsire—father of a horse's dam or sire; "grandfather."

granuloma [*gran-you-low´-muh*]—excessive non-healing tissue in a wound.

gravel—an acute infection occurring beneath the white line of the hoof; can cause severe lameness.

gravid [*graa´-vid*]—pregnant.

gray—a haircoat that is a mixture of black and white hairs; dappled gray has mottling or spots in a darker or lighter shade.

grazing bit—a traditional western curb bit with short shanks that angle backward so that they will drag on the ground while the horse grazes.

green (also "green broke")—untrained or inexperienced horse.

grey—see **gray**

grinding teeth—form of resistance to the bit.

groom (also "lad" "girl" "swipe")—*(n)* term for the person responsible for the daily care and exercise of horses; *(v)* to bathe, clip, brush, and generally clean a horse.

groom room—at a show, a stall used for grooming and preparing the horse for a class.

grooming—bathing, clipping, cleaning and brushing.

ground driving (also "ground work" "ground training" "long-reining" "long-lining")—conditioning and training exercise where the horse is driven by the handler from the ground.

ground line—a pole on the ground set at the base of a jump; allows the horse to see and gauge the distance better.

ground tie—a maneuver where the end of the lead rope is dropped to the ground, the horse stands perfectly still, and pays attention to the handler where ever he may be.

ground training—see **ground work**

ground work (also "ground training")—see **long-lining** and **lunging**

gullet—the open area on the underside of a saddle, directly under the seat.

gut sounds—the noises heard in a horse's abdomen; used to determine the possibility of, or state of, colic or intestinal motility.

gut strangulation—death of part of the large intestine as a result of lack of blood supply to the affected area, usually from a twisted bowel.

gutteral pouch—a sac-like enlargement of the lower end of the ear canals; unique to horses.

gymkhana [*jim-kan´-uh*]—an event consisting of games for horses and riders.

H

HCG—see **Human Chorionic Gonadatropin**

HYPP—see **Hyperkalemic Periodic Paralysis**

habit—see **riding habit**

hackamore (also "jaquima")—a bitless bridle that works on the horse's nose and jaw, but not its mouth; used for training young horses, or for horses with injured or tender mouths.

hacking—pleasure riding.

half-brother, sister—horses produced by the same dam, but a different sire.

half-halt—slight reining back.

half-passage [*haf pa-sahj´*]—diagonal movement forward and sideways, with the outside leg crossing over the inside leg.

half-stockings—white marking that only reaches to the mid-cannon bone.

halter—1) (*n*) (also "headcollar") a webbing or leather headstall without a bit or reins; 2) (*v*) to put a halter on a horse; 3) in racing, slang for claiming a horse.

halter class—a class in which horses are judged on looks, conformation, conditioning, and way of going.

halter horse—a horse that is suitable to be shown at halter or in-hand in conformation or model classes.

halter prospect—a horse that is deemed to have good potential to show in-hand in conformation or model classes.

hame draft (also "hame draught")—in driving, the projection on the hame through which the traces run.

hame strap—the strap that connects the hames.

hames—two rigid pieces on the sides of a horse collar, that act as guides or holders for the traces.

hand—4 inches; the unit used for measuring the height of horses from the withers to the ground.

hand-breeding—a mating where the mare and stallion are controlled by handlers, rather than being allowed to breed at will naturally.

hand-gallop—a gait that is faster than a canter, but slightly slower than a full gallop.

hand-graze—allow a horse to graze while haltered or controlled by a handler.

handicap—(*n*) in racing, when weights are carried to make all the horses evenly matched; (*v*) to select horses based on their past performances on the track.

handicapper—one who determines the weight that horses will carry in handicap races.

handler—see **exhibitor** or **trainer**

"hard mouth"—a horse that requires heavy or forceful rein control to ride or drive.

"hard keeper"—a horse that requires more food than is usual to stay fit.

hardware (also "fittings")—the metal parts used on tack, such as bits, chains, snaps, etc.

"Hark back"—term used when the hounds come out of the covert.

harness—the equipment (tack) used for hitching and driving a horse.

harness training—training a horse to be driven.

haunches—the collective term used to describe the hip, quarter and thigh of the horse.

Havana color—a medium brown saddlery color.

hay bag—a suspended mesh, canvas or net bag for feeding hay in a trailer or stall away from home.

hay rack—a wooden or metal feeding rack bolted permanently to the stall wall.

head bumper (also "poll guard")—a protective helmet for use with high-headed horses or in low-ceilinged trailers.

head carriage (also "head set")—the position of the horse's head when it responds to the bit.

head check—the part of the harness bridle that is used to control the head set.

headcollar—see **halter**

head set—see **head carriage**

head-shy—term used for a horse that fears or dislikesbeing touched around the head.

head stall—see **bridle**

header—1) in driving, the person who handles the horse's head while the driver is making adjustments or is outside of the carriage; in showing, the header enters the ring at the line-up and stands at the horse's head while the entries are judged; 2) in team roping, the partner who ropes the horns of the steer.

heads—the two pommel horns on a side saddle.

heat—(*n*) 1) (also "in heat" or "in season") term used to describe the time that a mare is receptive to the stallion; estrus; 2) in (harness) racing, a race where more than one running decides the winner.

heaves (also "broken wind" or "emphysema")—a disease of the respiratory system in horses (similar to emphysema in humans) involving rupture of the alveolar walls; symptoms include chronic cough, lack of stamina, and formation of a ridge, or heave line on the belly due to prolonged abdominal muscle contractions.

heavy horse—see **draft horse**

heel—the back of the hoof.

heel crack (also "sand crack")—a crack of the hoof wall at the heel.

heel nerve—see **nerving**

heel spot—white spot on one heel.

heeler—in team roping, the partner who ropes the legs of the steer.

hematoma [*hee-muh-toe´-muh*]—a bruise, usually accompanied by swelling.

hemoglobin—the pigment of red blood cells that carries oxygen.

hemolytic icterus—a fatal condition in newborn foals caused by an accidental mixing of the the foal's blood with the mare's; the mare's body produces antibodies to the "intruder" blood and, as the foal nurses, these antibodies are passed on through the colostrum, destroying the foal's blood and causing death if not treated.

hemophilia [*hee-mow-fill´-ee-uh*]—free bleeding as a result of an inherited abnormality of the clotting mechanism.

hemorrhage [*hem´-or-age*]—excessive bleeding.

hemospermia [*hee-mow-sper´-mee-uh*]—blood in the semen.

herbal—of or pertaining to herbs.

herbology—the study of herbs and their medicinal uses.

herd—the natural grouping of a band of horses.

herd bound—unwilling to be away from the herd for any reason.

herd instinct—the built-in desire for horses to band together for safety.

hereditary—being inherited from parents or ancestors.

heritability—the likelihood that a trait can be inherited.

heritability estimate—the term for assessing the probability that a trait will be passed from parents to offspring.

Hermes saddle—see **saddle, English; close-contact**

herpesvirus [*her´-pees-vy-rus*]—a group of viruses; one causes equine rhinopneumonitis.

heterosis [*heh-ter-oh´-sis*]—beneficial effects on vigor, fertility, and growth as a result of crossing different species or types (hybridization).

heterozygous [*heh-ter-oh-zy´-gus*]—hybrid; having two different alleles at a single locus on the chromosome.

hierarchy [*high´-er-ark-ee*]—the order of rank from highest to lowest; in a herd of horses it is known as the "pecking order."

high-headed—term for horses that have a very erect head carriage.

high school airs (also "airs above the ground")—in dressage, movements performed with either fore, hind, or all four feet off the ground.

high spavin—see **bone spavin**

hilltopper (also "point rider")—in hunting, a rider who follows the hunt from points to the rear of the field.

hindquarters—the parts of the horse behind the barrel.

hindquarters engaged—movement where the hindlegs of the horse are well under the body and show good flexion of the joints.

hindquarters leading or trailing—in dressage, in the half-pass, the hindquarters are ahead of the forehand or have been left behind.

hinny—offspring produced by a stallion and a female donkey (jennet).

hip strap—the strap on harness that supports the breeching.

hippomanes—small lumps of tissue that attach the placenta to the uterine wall.

histamine—a naturally-occurring chemical in the body that is released during allergic reactions.

hitch—1) *(n)* term for a team or pair of horses that are used together for driving; (see also **unicorn, tandem, four-in-hand**) 2) *(v,)* to attach a horse or team to a driving vehicle.

hitched (also "hooked" "hooked up" "in draft/draught")—attached to a driving vehicle by a harness and equipment.

hitching up—attaching the horse or team to the driving vehicle.

"hittin' a lick"—popular term describing a Tennessee Walking Horse that is showing good high action.

hobbles (also "hopples")—straps or ropes used to prevent kicking, or wandering off in the case of an untied horse; **breeding h.**—used to prevent a mare from kicking the stallion during breeding; **grazing h.**—in ranching or trail riding, used to prevent working horses from wandering away while not being used; **Scotch h.**—a soft cotton rope tied to the halter, then down and around one pastern with a quick-release knot; used to teach horses to ground-tie.

hock—the hind leg equivalent of the elbow.

hogging—see **roaching**

holdback—see **breeching**

holistic—a term meaning "the whole."

hollow back (also "sway back")—a concave top outline, often seen in old horses.

homebred—a horse that is bred by its owner.

homeopathy—a form of holistic medicine in which remedies are derived from plants, animals, and minerals

homing instinct—the built-in desire of horses to be in a familiar place where they feel safe and are fed.

homozygous—purebred; having two identical alleles at a single locus on the chromosome.

hood—a head covering used along with a blanket for added warmth.

hoof—common term for the horse's foot.

hoof black (also "hoof polish")—a shiny black polish that is applied to the dark feet of show horses before a class.

hoof bound—term for lameness caused by contraction of the hoof wall.

hoof dressing (also "hoof black" or "hoof polish")—a shiny polish, either black or clear for white feet, applied for appearance; some dressings also have beneficial elements that strengthen the hoof wall or protect it from damage.

hoof packing—a claylike material that is applied to the bottom of the foot.

hoof pick—a device for cleaning out the underside of the hoof.

hoof polish—see **hoof dressing**

hoof tester—a tool resembling ice-tongs that is used to test for tender spots in the hoof by applying pressure in various places.

hoof wall—the hard outer portion of the hoof.

hooked or **hooked up**—see **hitched**

hopples—see **hobbles**

horn—1) one of two extensions of the mare's uterus; 2) the "handle" on a western saddle, used for tying a rope during roping.

horny frog—a non-sensitive structure on the bottom of the hoof that serves as a shock absorber, traction device, and circulation aid.

horny sole—a non-sensitive structure located on the bottom of the foot; it protects the sensitive sole and the other parts above it, as well as providing traction.

horny wall—the outermost layer of the hoof.

horse—1) a male horse over the age of three; 2) member of species *Equus caballus;* 3) an equine over 14.2 hands high.

horse box—see **trailer**

horse brass—decorative brass designs used on heavy horse harness.

horseshoer—see **farrier**

horsing—see **estrus**

hot iron—traditional branding iron used for marking livestock.

hot-bloods—term for horses such as Arabian or Barb; this type developed in the southern regions where survival depended on the ability to exist on less food and water; characterized by speed, endurance, and fine body structure.

hot-walker—1) a stable helper who walks horses after exercise to cool them out; 2) a motorized, freely rotating umbrella-shaped structure with rings attached to the "ribs"; horses are tied to a "rib" and are "led" in a circle at a designated rate of speed; allows several horses to cooled out at one time.

Human Chorionic Gonadatropin (HCG) [*kor-ee-on´-ik goe-nad-oh-trow´-pin*]—a human hormone that stimulates ovulation in the mare when given at the right time.

hunt boot—a low-heeled English style riding boot reaching to just below the knee and sometimes having a cuff at the top.

hunt cap—protective headwear for English riding and jumping; usually black velvet with a chin strap.

hunt seat—see **forward seat**

hunter-type (also "hunter")—long, lean, rangy horses with good muscles and long legs; these animals move with long, low strides and exhibit speed, fluidity, and jumping ability; they usually are taller and lighter than other horses and carry the head lower.

hunting whip—a practical riding aid carried in the field; one end has a crook handle for opening gates and the other has long lashes for controlling the hounds.

huntmaster—see **Master of Fox Hounds**

huntsman—in hunting, the person that has charge of all kennel activities and is in charge of the hounds in the field.

hurdle horse—see **jumper**

hurrying—losing rhythm by starting to rush.

husbandry—farming; animal farming.

hybrid—the offspring of two individuals with different genotypes; i.e., a mare mated to a jack donkey produces a mule.

hybrid vigor—when two individuals are crossed and the resulting offspring is superior in vigor, size, and resistance to either parent.

hybridization—producing hybrids.

hydrated—infused with water.

hydrocephalus—water in the brain cavity where brain tissue should be.

Hyperkalemic Periodic Paralysis (also "HYPP")—a genetic disease, primarily of Quarter Horses, which results in episodes of muscle tremors, stiffness, and paralysis.

hypersensitivity—excessively sensitive to something.

hypothalmus—a part of the brain that regulates many body functions.

hypothyroidism—reduced thyroid hormone production.

hypertrophy [*high-per´-trow-fee*]—increase in size of an organ or tissue.

IM—medical abbreviation for *intramuscular*, meaning "into a muscle."

IV—medical abbreviation for *intravenous*, meaning "into a vein."

icing—see **cryotherapy**

icterus—see **jaundice**

idiopathic [*ih-dee-oh-path´-ik*]—of unknown origin.

immune system—that which controls an organism's susceptibility to disease.

immunity—having resistance to disease.

immunization—vaccination; the administration of antibodies to particular diseases.

immunologic—pertaining to the immune system.

immunotherapy—treating lack of immunity with measured doses of a particular disease so that the body will form antibodies and its own immunity.

impaction—blockage of the intestines, similar to constipation, that causes colic.

impinge—striking or touching another object.

impotency—in a stallion, the inability or lack of interest to breed.

imprint—1) to fix or implant firmly training or commands in the mind or memory of a horse; 2) a foal will imprint, or "memorize" its dam.

impulsion—forward motion.

in draught [*draft*]—see **hitched**

"in frame"—the balance of a horse; the way it stands or moves over its legs.

in-gate—the entrance to a show arena or ring.

in hand—1) showing a horse at halter in a conformation class; 2) in racing, under moderate control-not at top speed.

"in harness" (also **"under harness"**)—being worked in harness; driven.

in heat—see **heat**

in season—see **heat**

"in the bridle"—see **"on the bit"**

"in the money"—a horse that finishes first, second, or third—the payoff placings.

in utero—within the uterus.

in vivo—within the living body.

"in wear"—term used to describe a horse's teeth when they have grown in completely through the gums and are touching the opposing teeth.

inbreeding—the mating of closely-related individuals or of individuals having similar genotypes.

independent seat—a rider that is able to ride in balance without reins or stirrups.

indirect rein—control accomplished by pressing slightly sideways on one side of the mouth, directing the horse to bend around a turn.

induced labor—artificial stimulation of uterine contractions using medications.

infantile—undeveloped or very young.

infection—having large numbers of microorganisms in the body.

infertile—reproductively inactive or non-productive.

infertility—(*n*) condition of being reproductively inactive or non-productive.

inflammation—a reaction to injury, infection or irritation characterized by redness, swelling, heat, and pain.

inflammatory—caused by or characterized by inflammation.

influenza—a viral infection characterized by inflammation of the respiratory tract, fever, and muscular pain.

inguinal [*ing´-gwih-nul*]—relating to the groin.

inherent—inborn or natural.

inherited lethal—gene passed from parent to offspring that will cause death of the embryo, fetus, or newborn.

innoculation—vaccination.

inquiry (see also **objection**)—in racing, a complaint lodged by a racing official.

insemination—introduction of semen into the vagina.

instinctive—natural reaction; not learned.

insult—term for trauma or disease invasion of the body.

interdental space (see also **bars**)—the area on the horse's jaws where there are no teeth, between the front and back teeth; the bit lies in this area on the lower jaw.

interference (see also **forging, over-reaching, cross-firing**)—gait abnormalities in which any foot is struck by another during movement.

intramuscular (IM)—into or within a muscle.

intrauterine—within the uterus.

intravenous (IV)—into or within a vein or vessel.

invert—turn inside out.

irons—metal English riding stirrups.

irregular strides—irregular rhythm of the pace.

isoerythrolysis [*eye-sow-air-rih-thral´-lih-sis*]—a condition similar to the Rh factor problem in humans, in which the foal produces antibodies to its own red blood cells, as a result of its blood mixing with the dam's during gestation.

isolate—remove from the whole.

isolation—removing diseased or possibly-exposed animals to a restricted area completely away from the rest of the stock.

ivermectin—a type of medication used for deworming horses.

 J

Jack spavin—see **bone spavin**

Japan—a black varnish-like covering that is used to finish metal or leather.

jaquima—see **hackamore**

jaundice (also "icterus")—having a yellow discoloration.

jerkline—in roping, a rope that runs from the bit shanks back through a ring or pulley at the horn, and is usually loosely tucked into the roper's belt; this rope pulls back as the calf-roper moves toward the calf in front of the horse.

jig—a prancing, non-gait that occurs when a horse makes a poor transition from a walk to a trot or from a trot to a walk.

jockey fee—see **fee**

jodhpurs [*jahd´-purrs*]—traditional riding pants with tight legs and fullness above the knee.

jodhpur boot (also "gaiter boot")—a low-heeled over-the-ankle riding boot with elastic sides, or side strap or zipper closure.

jog (also "jog trot")—1) in western riding, the same as the trot; 2) in driving, a slow trot.

jog cart—see **cart**

jog trot—see **jog**

joint capsule—the cartilage surrounding a joint.

jointed curb (also "Tom Thumb")—a short-shanked curb bit that is sometimes confused with a snaffle because of the jointed mouthpiece.

jowl—the fleshy underportion of the jaw.

jowl wrap—(see also **neck sweat**) a heat-producing wrap to remove excess fluid from the throatlatch area and top of the neck behind the poll.

jump (see also **fence**)—in jumping, any obstacle erected on the course.

jump course designer—an individual who designs a course for jumping and supervises its construction.

jump cup—the adjustable holder for the bars of a jump.

jump standard—the pole or base on either side of the jump.

jumper—a hurdle horse or steeplechaser.

jumpoff—in show jumping, a test to determine a winner by elimination.

junior exhibitor (also "youth")—in showing, an exhibitor under 18 years of age (may vary depending on sanctioning organization).

junior horse—for showing purposes, a horse that is between two and four years old.

juniors—in combined training, an exhibitor up to the age of 18 years.

juvenile—a two-year-old horse.

K

keepers—leather holders on tack that secure adjustable pieces to keep them from flapping.

Kentucky jodhpurs—riding pants similar to traditional jodhpurs, but with a flared cuff; used in saddleseat attire.

keratin [*care´-uh-tin*]—a protein which is the chief component of hair, nails, etc.

keratoma [*care-uh-tow´-muh*]—a tumor-like growth in the hoof wall that exerts pressure on the laminae, causing lameness.

kick strap—in driving, a strap attached to the shafts that runs up and across the horse's croup, side to side; prevents bucking or kicking.

kicking boots—padded boots used on the back legs to reduce damage of a kick.

killed virus—a vaccine prepared from suspensions of chemically-killed viruses; produces passive immunity.

"killers"—butchers that process horses for meat.

Kimbelwicke bit—a variation on the Pelham bit that looks like a short-shanked curb; preferred for beginner riders or jumping riders that don't want to deal with double reins.

knackers—see **killers**

knee boot—see **boot**

knee sprung—see **over at the knee**

knee strap—a type of restraint using a leather strap that slips over the pastern and then pulled up and buckled around the forearm, leaving the horse standing on three legs.

knock knees—conformation default where the knees deviate toward each other.

Kur—dressage performed to music; a musical freestyle.

 L

LH—see **Luteinizing Hormone**

labia [*lay´-bee-uh*]—the vertical lips on either side of the opening of the vulva.

lactating—producing milk.

lactational anestrus [*lack-tay´-shun-al ann-es´-trus*]—failure to show heat after foaling.

ladies—adult female exhibitors.

"lad"—see **groom**

lair—see **earth**

lame—term for a horse with an abnormal gait, usually due to pain.

laminitis [*lamb-in-eye´-tus*] (also "founder")—inflammation of the laminae in the horse's foot; crippling condition of the feet that is caused mainly by overeating, severe overwork on hard ground, or bacterial infection (such as post-foaling founder).

lap robe—see **driving apron**

lariat [*lair´-ee-at*] (also "lasso")—a rope with a running noose.

"lark"—hunting term for jumping fences when out on a non-hunting day, or when the hounds are not running.

laryngeal paresis [*lair´-in-jeel pair-ee´-sus*]—see **roaring**

laryngitis—inflammation of the larynx, causing hoarseness.

larynx [*lair´-inks*]—the voice box.

lashes—thin strips of leather or other material attached to the end of various whips for the purpose of making a noise when snapped.

lasso—(*v*) to rope and catch an animal; (*n*) (see **lariat**).

late change—in a flying change, the front and hind lead legs do not change simultaneously.

late double—see **daily double**

lateral—to the side or along the side.

lateral cartilage—elastic structures in the hoof, located on both sides of the coffin bone; these function to reduce concussion.

lateral cartilage necrosis—see **quittor**

lateral movements—movements requiring sideways motion in addition to forward motion.

lathered—see **washed out**

latigo—a lightweight headstall that attaches to a hackamore.

lavage—medical term for "washing out" by flushing with water.

lead [*leed*]—1) (*n*) (also "shank" "rope") a sturdy rope or line, 5-6 feet in length, with a snap attachment at one end or a length of chain and snap at one end; 2) sequence of legs during a canter which describes which foreleg strikes the ground first.

lead change—changing the leading legs of the front and rear pairs, at a lope or canter, when changing the direction of travel.

leading rein—the rein pulled to signal the horse to turn to that side.

lead rope—see **lead**

lead shank—see **lead**

lease—(*v*) to "rent" a horse for a contracted period of time; (*n*) the terms stipulated and agreed upon for the rental or use of a horse.

leathers—the leather straps by which stirrups are lengthened or shortened.

leg up—assistance from the ground in mounting a horse.

leg wraps—bandages used on the legs for either therapeutic, preventive, or cosmetic reasons.

legume [*leh-goom´*]—a hay such as alfalfa, trefoil, or clover; these plants manufacture nitrogen while growing.

lesion—injury or damage that results in impairment or loss of function.

let down—1) to gradually stop training; 2) in the mare, when she allows the milk to flow.

lethal gene—an inherited gene that will cause death in an embryo, fetus, newborn, or even mature individual.

Lethal White Foal Syndrome (also "White Foal Syndrome")—an inherited disorder associated with the overo color pattern; the foal is born with limited pigmentation and cannot pass food through the gut due to either closure of the intestine (atresia coli) or lack of nerve cells which control intestinal peristalsis.

lethargic [*leh-thar´-jik*]—sluggish and sleepy; without any vigor.

leukocytes [*loo´-koh-sites*]—white blood cells that fight infection.

leverage—control attained by using a shank bit to multiply the pressure that the rider uses on the reins.

liberty class—in some breed shows, a class where a stallion is turned loose in an enclosed arena and allowed to run freely accompanied by music; the horse must be caught and haltered within a certain time limit in order to be judged.

libido [*lih-bee´-doe*]—the urge or desire to mate.

ligament—a tough fibrous band connecting or supporting bone, cartilage, or muscle.

light horse—fine-boned, medium sized horse such as Arabian, Morgan, Quarter, or Thoroughbred.

light rein—allowing a little sag to the reins, but maintaining contact with the horse's mouth.

line—in hunting, the scent trail of a fox.

linebreeding—a conservative program of inbreeding designed to concentrate the blood of a certain ancestor within the linebred offspring.

linecrossing—a breeding program that mates individuals from two distinct families.

line-up—in showing, when all exhibitors line up in the center of the ring for the judges' final look and placing.

lines—in driving, the term for reins.

liniment—a medicated liquid for topical use on strains and sprains.

listlessness—having no interest in what is going on.

live bacterial suspension—a vaccine that contains living bacteria capable of causing disease; it produces longer-lasting active immunity.

"live foal"—in breeding, term for a foal who stands and nurses on its own.

"live foal guarantee"—a guarantee made by the stallion owner that provides for a live foal as the result of a purchased breeding.

live unmodified virus—a vaccine that can cause a mild form of disease, but produces very effective immunity.

livery—1) the uniform worn by various riding and driving professionals; 2) the keeping and feeding of horses for a fee (also "stable"); 3) horses and/or vehicles for hire.

loafing shed—see **run-in shed**

locus—site of an allele on a chromosome.

lockjaw—see **Tetanus**

loins—between the back and the point of the hip on either side of the spine.

London color—a light golden-brown saddlery color.

long reining—see **ground driving**

longe—see **lunge**

longeing cavesson—see **lunging cavesson**

longe line—see **lunge line**

longe roller—see **surcingle**

longe whip—see **lunge whip**

longeing—see **lunging**

loose rein—putting no pressure on the bit unless the reins are pulled.

lope—the western gait equivalent of the canter.

loriner [*lore´-in-er*]—a maker of bits, stirrups, spurs and other metal saddlery items.

lunge [*lunj*] (also "longe")—to exercise a horse at the end of a long line attached to the halter; horse is trotted and cantered in a circle going both directions of the circle.

lunge line (also "longe line")—a very long lead line (20-30 feet) used for exercising a horse in a circle through various gaits.

lunge roller—see **surcingle**

lunge whip (also "longe whip")—a training aid that is 6 to 7 feet long with long lashes at the tip; used to keep the horse out at the end of the lunge line.

lunging [*lun´-jing*] (also "longeing" "tethered work")—early training in which the trainer directs the horse at the end of a lunge line to move through the gaits in a circle; this conditions the horse and teaches it obedience to voice commands.

lunging cavesson—a headstall fitted with rings across the nose band, to which the lunge line is attached.

luteal tissue [*loo´-tee-ul*]—matter that fills the ruptured follicle after the egg has been released.

Luteinizing Hormone [*loo´-tee-in-eye-zing*]—hormone produced by the pituitary that stimulates the development of corpora lutea in the mare.

luxating—loose.

Lyme Disease—a serious disease transmitted to horses and humans by deer ticks; causes lameness, fever, eye irritation, and other flu-like symptoms.

lymphocytes [*lim´-foh-sites*]—white blood cells that fight disease.

lyse [*lice*]—degenerate or disintegrate.

lysine [*lie´-seen*]—an essential amino acid needed in the diet of a growing horse.

 M

MFH—see **Master of Fox Hounds**

maiden class—a class for a horse that has not won a blue ribbon in approved competition or race.

maiden horse—a horse that has not won a blue ribbon in approved competition or race.

maiden mare—a mare that has never been bred.

malabsorption—the inability of the intestines to absorb nutrients.

malformations—abnormal formations.

malignant—severe affliction, resisting treatment, usually fatal, sometimes with uncontrolled growth, as in a tumor.

malleable [*may´-lee-uh-bul*]—workable, easy to handle.

malocclusion [*mal-oh-klew´-shun*]—when teeth do not fit properly together to grind food.

malpositioned—incorrectly positioned, especially in foaling.

mammary—pertaining to the milk-secreting glands of the mare.

manége [*man-ayzh´*]—a riding academy.

mandibles—the jaws.

mane—the long hair that grows along the entire length of the neck of the horse.

mane tamer (also "mane trainer")—a neck wrap used to train an unruly mane to lie flat.

manger—a wooden box or crib for feeding hay.

manifest—show up or become evident.

manners—a horse's interaction with humans and other horses.

manure (also "feces")—term for solid waste produced by livestock.

mare—an adult female horse.

mark—see **marking**

mark to ground—in foxhunting, the barking signal of the hounds that they have run the fox to its lair.

marking—any of various shapes or patterns of white on a solid color coat; **face m.**-white hair in shape of star, blaze, snip, strip, etc. on the face; **leg m.**-white hair in various shapes: anklet, sock, stocking, coronet, etc. over the legs.

martingale—a training device used to control the position of the horse's head. **bib m.**-triangular piece of leather between two forked chest straps; prevents horses from catching their feet in the tack; **running m.**-strap that attaches to girth, runs up between the front legs and splits into two straps with rings at the ends, through which the reins run; when the horse raises his head, the martingale pulls down on the reins and bit, pulling on the mouth; **standing m.**-a strap that attaches at the girth, runs between the front legs, up to the noseband, putting pressure on the horse's head when he raises it too high; **tie-down**-western term for standing martingale.

mash—a hot or cold mixture of grain and other feed that is moistened to make it soft and digestible.

mask—the head of the fox.

Master of Fox Hounds (MFH) (also "huntmaster")—in foxhunting, the individual who leads the field.

mastitis—inflammation of the mare's mammary glands.

maternal—on the mother's side.

Meadowbrook—an old-fashioned 2-wheeled country driving vehicle.

mecate [*meh-kah´-tay*]—a rope made of horsehair, cow tail, or mohair; used as the rein on a hackamore bridle.

mechanical hackamore—a potentially severe leverage-type hackamore that acts like a curb bit, but works on the nose and chin.

meconium [*mee-cone´-ee-um*]—the foal's first stool, consisting of digested fetal fluids, glandular secretions and mucus.

medial—at the center or centrally.

mediated—between two items.

meet—in hunting, the place where the hunting day begins.

meiosis [*my-oh´-sis*]—cell division.

melanin [*mel´-uh-nin*]—pigment granules in hair coat, eyes, skin, other tissues.

melanoma [*mel-uh-noh´-mah*]—a tumor of pigment cells.

metabolic—pertaining to the transformation of energy into a usable form.

metabolism—the process by which all living organisms convert nourishment into energy and waste.

metastasize [*meh-tas´-tuh-size*]—spread of disease throughout the organism.

metritis [*meh-try´-tus*]—inflammation of the uterus.

microchip—a tiny chip containing identification information that can be implanted under a horse's skin.

migratory—pattern of movement.

milk replacer—a liquid milk formula for foals.

modified live virus—a vaccine prepared from suspensions of live virus particles; these vaccines stimulate antibody formation by causing a mild case of the disease.

model class—see **halter class**

Monday-morning sickness—see **azoturia**

monkey mouth—see **prognathism**

monorchidism [*mon-or´-kid-izm*]—complete absence of one or both testicles.

montura—see **saddle, western; Peruvian**

moon blindness—see **periodic ophthalmia**

morbidity—infection rate.

mortality—death.

motility—normal, forward movement.

mount—1) (*n*) a horse that is ridden; 2) (*v*) the act of getting up into the saddle.

mounting block—a step or block on the ground for use in mounting a very tall horse.

mountings (also "furniture")—in driving, the hardware used on harness.

mouth—term for the way a horse handles a bit in its mouth.

move off—to start a gait from a standstill.

muck-bucket—a large tub with rope handles; used for collecting manure during stall cleaning.

"mucking out"—cleaning stalls.

mucopurulent [*mew-ko-pure´-you-lent*]—bacteria-laden mucus resulting from infection.

mucous [*mew´-cuss*]—(*adj.*) having the ability to excrete a lubricating secretion, *mucus.*

mucous membrane—a membrane that secretes mucus.

mucus [*mew´-cuss*]—(*n*) the lubricating excretion of a mucous membrane.

mud brush—see **dandy brush**

mud cracks—see **scratches**

mud lark—see **mudder**

mud scraper—a grooming tool used for removing encrusted mud from the legs and under belly.

mudder (also "mudlark")—a horse that races well on muddy tracks.

mule—cross between a mare and a jack (male donkey).

multiple modality—using several forms of treatment at the same time.

murmur—a sound heard in the heart.

mutation—sudden and permanent change in an individual's genotype.

mutton withers—low withers.

muzzle—1) the horse's nose and lips; 2) a device that covers the nose and mouth to prevent eating, biting, chewing, or wind-sucking (cribbing).

 N

NI—see **Neonatal Isoerythrolysis**

NMS—see **Neonatal Maladjustment Syndrome**

nag—slang term for a horse, especially in racing circles.

nasal—pertaining to the nose or nostrils.

natural aid—see **aids**

natural selection—"survival of the fittest" concept, resulting in elimination of weak or inferior individuals from the breeding pool.

navicular bone [*nuh-vih´-kew-lur*]—the bone located between the coffin bone and underneath the short pastern bone; functions as a fulcrum point for the deep flexor tendon.

navicular disease—degenerative disease and changes in the navicular bones, causing lameness.

near side—the left side of the horse; all mounting, saddling, bridling, etc. take place on this side.

neatsfoot oil—an oil obtained by boiling the feet and shinbones of cattle; used for dressing leather.

neck rein—in western riding, putting the opposite rein against the horse's neck toward the direction you want to go; a horse must be trained to neck rein.

neck rope—in roping, a rope around the horse's neck through which the catch rope is threaded and then tied to the saddle; acts as a guide for the horse to move back.

neck sweat—a heat-producing wrap that reduces bulk due to water retention.

necrosis [*neh-kroh'-sis*]—death of tissue.

neigh—the vocalization of a horse.

neonatal [*nee-oh-nay'-tul*]—pertaining to the newborn.

Neonatal Isoerythrolysis (NI) [*eye'-sew-air-rih-thrah'-lih-sus*]—a potentially lethal condition in which a foal has somehow acquired blood from the dam during delivery or trauma; the foal receives the mare's antibodies through the colostrum and begins to produce antibodies to its own blood cells; treatable if diagnosed early.

Neonatal Maladjustment Syndrome (NMS)—a serious condition of newborn foals thought to be caused by reduced blood flow during delivery; foals become disoriented, unable to nurse, stand by themselves, and eventually die without veterinary intervention.

neonate—a newborn.

neoplasm—tumor; abnormal, rapid tissue growth.

nerving (also "heel nerve" or "neurectomy")—surgical removal of the nerve supply to the navicular area of the foot.

neurectomy—see **nerving**

neurologic [*nur-oh-lah'-jik*]—having a basis pertaining to the nervous system.

neuromuscular—pertaining to the muscles and nerves.

New Zealand rug—a heavy horseblanket that has a canvas covering.

Newmarket boot—a waterproof English-style tall riding boot.

nick (also "click")—crossing well with certain individuals.

nicker—a soft, throaty sound that a horse makes.

"night eyes"—see **chestnut**

nine-day heat—see **foal heat**

nocturnal—pertaining to night.

nonspermicidal—an agent that will not harm or destroy sperm.

noseband—part of the bridle used to prevent the horse from evading the bit by opening his mouth; **curb n.**-a severe style noseband connected with chains to the curb bit hooks; **chain n.**-a leather-wrapped chain replaces the regular noseband; **drop n.**-noseband that exerts pressure on the nose, producing lower head carriage; **figure-8 n.** (also "Grackle")-double straps criss-cross the horse's nose and buckle under the chin; **flash n.**-a second noseband attached above the horse's nose, buckling underneath the chin below the bit; keeps the horse's mouth closed; **Kineton n.**-a drop noseband for use on very strong horses that pull; the nosepiece comes into direct contact with the bit; **rope-front n.**-a leather-wrapped rope replaces the regular noseband; **spike or spike-nose n.**-a very severe noseband with small metal studs in the lining that rest against the horse's skin.

nose-clamp—see **twitch, humane**

"not straight"—see **crooked**

novice—a person who is new to showing or exhibiting; a beginner.

novice class—a class open to novice exhibitors or novice horses.

novice horse—1) in eventing, a horse that has never competed above the Training Level; 2) in showing, a horse that has not won 3 blue ribbons in a division.

novice rider—in eventing, a rider who has not competed above the Training Level.

nucleus—the structure in the cell that contains DNA.

nurse mare—a mare that is chosen for her good mothering instincts, then bred each year for the purpose of raising orphan foals.

 O

objection (see also **protest**)—a complaint or claim by a rider, judge, or official.

obstacle course—a class having several specific obstacles that must be negotiated in a certain order or in a certain amount of time.

occult [*ah-kult'*]—hidden or concealed.

ocular [*ah'-kew-lur*]—pertaining to the eye.

occult spavin (also "blind spavin")—calcification formed on the adjacent bone surface in the hock; it prevents normal movement; there is no external sign of the condition.

off course—when the horse moves out of the designated pattern in an event or takes a jump in the wrong order.

off side (also "far side")—the right side of the horse.

"off the hocks"—leg conformation in which the hocks are too far back.

off track betting—the placing of parimutuel racing bets at licensed betting parlors rather than at the racetrack.

offset knees—a conformation fault in which the leg does not follow a straight line through the radius and cannon bones.

offspring (also "progeny")—the product of a mating.

oiling—administering mineral oil through a nose tube into the stomach to help pass blockage; sometimes used before long trailer trips to prevent colic.

olfactory [*ohl'-fak-tree*]—pertaining to the sense of smell.

Olympic saddle—see **saddle, English; close-contact**

on course—the area within which the horse and rider must stay during an equestrian event.

"on the bit" (also "in the bridle")—1) in racing, when a horse is eager to run; 2) in showing, when the horse is in control and attentive.

"on the board"—in racing, finishing in the first three places.

"on the forehand"—when the head is low and forward, with most of the weight on the front legs.

"on the muscle"—1) term for a horse that is fit and conditioned; 2) term for a horse that is being pushy or aggressive.

on the rail—1) in showing, when the horse is traveling next to the barrier that surrounds the arena; 2) in racing, when the horse is next to the inside rail, which is the shortest distance around the track.

on the vertical—in riding, describes the position of the rider when a vertical line can be drawn through the ear, shoulder, point of the hip, and the heel.

one track—in dressage, the hindfeet follow in the footsteps of the forefeet.

open—not in foal.

open horse—see "**big lick horse**"

open show—a show that allows anyone to enter, regardless of the breed of horse they are exhibiting.

opening rein—see **direct rein**

ophthalmic [*off-thal'-mik*]—pertaining to the eyes.

oral—by mouth.

orchitis [*or-kite'-is*]—inflammation of the testicles.

orofacial [*or-oh-fay'-shul*]—having to do with the mouth and face.

osselets (*also spelled osslets*)—lesions that affect the fetlock joint, usually caused by a torn fibrous joint capsule.

ossification [*ah-sih-fih-kay'-shun*]—forming or changing into bone.

osteoarthritis—joint degeneration and inflammation due to excess wear.

osteochondritis (also "epiphysitis" "osteochondrosis" "subchondral cyst")—in young growing horses, the conversion of cartilage to bone in the long bones is disturbed.

osteochondrosis—see **osteochondritis**

osteoporosis—a condition where bones become very porous and brittle.

"ouchy"—having a sore foot or tender feet.

out of—born; referring to the mare's delivery.

"out of the money"—in racing, a horse that finishes fourth or worse.

outbreeding (*not in current use*; see **outcrossing**)—breeding unrelated individuals to each other.

outcrossing—breeding two individuals who have no common ancestors for 5 generations or more.

outside—referring to the side of the horse that is closest to the rail.

outside horses—in a breeding/boarding facility, horses owned by other people.

outside mare—a mare to be bred that is not one of a breeding farm's own mares.

ovariectomy [*oh-vee-uh-rek'-toe-mee*]—removal of one or both ovaries.

ovaries—two gonads in the mare that produce the eggs and reproductive hormones; contain germinal cells.

"over at the knee" (also "buck knees" "goat knees" "knee sprung")—conformation fault where the knee is in front of the vertical.

overbent (also "behind the bit")—the horse's nose is behind the vertical as it bends its neck, which brings the head too close to the chest.

overcheck—on a bridle, the strap that goes from the bit, up over the nose, face, and poll, and attaches to the harness saddle.

overgirth—in racing, dressage, eventing, and driving, an elastic strap that goes completely around the horse and saddle to prevent the saddle from moving or slipping.

overlap time—when two or more feet are on the ground simultaneously; a shorter overlap time indicates that the horse travels faster because he spends less time on the ground.

overreach boot—see **boots, quarter**

over-reaching—a form of "interference"; term that describes the hind toe striking the bulb or heel of the front foot during movement.

overo [*oh-vair'-oh*]—a parti-color horse with four solid-color legs and white body body markings in irregular patterns from the underpart of the horse upwards, but not crossing over the back.

overshot jaw—see **brachygnathism**

ovulation [*ah-view-lay'-shun*]—the release of the egg from the ovary.

ovum [*oh'-vum*] (*pl. ova*)—egg.

oxer—a type of spread-jump for testing horizontal distance.

oxytocin [*ox-ih-toe'-sun*]—the hormone that stimulates uterine contractions.

 P

PGF2a—see **Prostaglandin F2alpha**

pace—1) a two-beat gait in which the fore and hind legs on each side move forward and backward at the same time; faster than the trot, but slower than the gallop; 2) the speed of a gait.

pack—1) (*n*) a group of hunting hounds; 2) (*v*) to carry supplies by horseback.

pack saddle—(also "sawbuck" "crossbuck") a combination of harness and saddle tree to which supplies can be secured.

pad—1) (also "saddle pad" "numnah") a soft cushion that is placed under the saddle to protect the horse's back, usually for jumping, trail riding, and other highly athletic events; 2) in driving, the saddle on harness.

pad cloth—see **coach housing**

paddling—faulty action of the front leg in which the foot swings to the outside.

paddock—1) fenced area for keeping a horse; 2) in racing, area where horses are saddled and paraded before a race.

paddock boot—a low-heeled, over-the-ankle riding boot with laces up the front.

paint—1) a counter-irritant containing iodine compounds; 2) common expression referring to a parti-colored horse.

palomino—1) a yellow colored haircoat over black skin, with white mane and tail; 2) a color breed of horse.

palpation—manual inspection of internal organs.

panel—1) the "cushion" on a saddle that sits between the saddle tree and the horse's back; 2) see **furlong**

panel fence—in jumping, a solid piece, usually slanted or up against a rail.

panic snap—a snap hook that will release if panic force is exerted.

panniers—oversize saddlebags used for pack horses.

papilloma [*pah-pih-low'-muh*]—a benign tumor with a fibrous center.

parade horse—a horse that has been trained to carry decorated tack, flags, and other unusual things in parades.

parade rest—a full, alert stop during a parade or drill maneuver.

paralysis—the condition of being unable to move.

parasite—any organism that lives off of another organism.

parimutuel betting—a system of betting where the winners divide the total amount wagered, based on the proportion of their wagers, after state and track shares are deducted.

park—in showing in saddleseat classes, a full, alert stop in the line-up; the horse is square over the front legs with the hind legs well behind.

park harness—in driving, a class for horses with showy, highly-animated action.

park horse—in showing, a horse that has been trained to perform a high-action trot with lots of brilliance; usually seen with Arabians, Morgans, Saddlebreds, Hackney Ponies, or Tennessee Walking Horses.

park trot—an exaggerated, very highly-animated trot.

parrot mouth—see **brachygnathism**

parti-colored (see also **piebald, overo, skewbald, tobiano**)—having more than one color in the hair coat, in definite patterns; i.e., appaloosa, pinto, etc.

parturition [*par-chur-ih'-shun*]—delivery or birth.

Passage [*pah-sahj'*]—a trot in which the horse moves with higher, more springy steps; one of the basic movements, or "Schools on the Ground," used in the Spanish Riding School.

passive flexion—a maneuver where the leg is flexed by the veterinarian or handler, rather than by the horse itself.

passive immunity—disease resistance acquired through the transfer of antibodies to the newborn.

pastern—the bone between the fetlock joint and the hoof.

pastern marking—white mark to the bottom of the ankle.

pasture—fenced-in land having grazing available.

pasture breeding—breeding system where the stallion is permanently turned out with the mares and allowed to tease and breed each mare as she comes into heat.

pasture rot—see **rain rot**

pasture rotation—pasture management system that moves livestock from one pasture to another regularly in order to preserve the forage and ground, and to allow parasite eggs to die off.

patella—the kneecap.

patent [*pay'-tent*]—open.

paternal—on the father's side.

pay off—see **dividend**

pecking order—see **hierarchy**

pectoral—pertaining to the chest.

pedal bone—*(not in current usage)* see **coffin bone**

pedal osteitis [*ahs-tee-eye'-tis*]—inflammation of the third phalanx (coffin bone) due to repetitive concussion on a thin sole, with resultant decalcification.

pedigree—an individual's ancestral history or "family tree."

Pelham bit [*pel'-um*]—a fused bit that is a combination of a curb and snaffle, having double action depending on which pair of reins are used.

penis—the male reproductive organ.

perfecta—see **exacta**

performance boot—see **boots**

performance prospect—a horse that is deemed to have good potential to show in performance classes; i.e., driving, riding, jumping, etc.

periocular [*pair-ee-ah'-kew-lur*]—around the eyes.

periodic opthalmia [*ahf-thal'-mee-uh*] (also "moon blindness")—a recurring inflammation of the internal eye.

periople—in the hoof, a sensitive structure that aids in retaining moisture in the foot.

periople ring—a sensitive structure that produces the periople; located just above the coronary band.

periosteum [*pair-ee-ah'-stee-um*]—the vascular membrane that covers and nourishes the bones.

periostitis (also "popped a splint" "bucked shins")—inflammation of the periosteum.

peripheral vision—seeing in a circular field surrounding the body.

peritonitis [*pair-ih-toe-nye'-tis*]—inflammation of the lining of the abdominal cavity or the lining of the organs therein.

perlino—a horse with pink skin, blue eyes, and a cream-colored haircoat with mane, tail, and lower legs sometimes a little darker; only a recognized color in some breeds.

Peruvian saddle—see **saddle, western**

phaeomelanin—see **pheomelanin**

Phaeton—a 4-wheeled vehicle drawn by one or two horses, having a folding top, and front and back seats.

phantom mare—see **dummy mare**

pharmacology—the study of drugs and their uses.

pharyngitis [*fair-in-jye'-tis*]—inflammation of the pharynx.

phenotype [*fee'-no-type*]—the visual outward appearance of an individual resulting from the interaction of its genotype and the environment.

phenylbutazone—see **bute**

pheomelanin [*fay-oh-mehl'-uh-nin*] (also "phaeomelanin")—the red or yellow form of melanin pigment granules.

pheromones [*fair'-oh-moans*]—body chemistry changes that are air-borne, indicating fear, excitement, and arousal.

photosensitive—sensitive to light.

physiology—the functions and vital processes of living organisms.

Piaffe [*pee'-ahf*]—a rhythmical trot while staying in one spot; one of the basic movements, or "Schools on the Ground," used in the Spanish Riding School.

picket line—in trail riding, a manner of tying horses to a strong rope stretched tightly between two or more trees; halter ropes are tied with quick-release knots to loops along the rope.

picking a stall—removing only the manure from the bedding, rather than turning or stripping the bedding; done daily.

piebald—a parti-color horse with a black haircoat patterned with white.

pig eyes—term for eyes that are small and round.

pigeon-toed—see **toe in**

piggin string—in roping, the string used to tie the animal.

pigment—coloring matter in cells and tissues.

pineal gland [*pie-neel'*]—part of the horse's brain that senses the amount of daylight through a nervous system connection with the eyes.

pinned—(also "placed" "tied")—in showing, awarded a ribbon.

pinto—1) common term for a parti-color horse; 2) a color breed of parti-color horse.

Pirouette [*peer-oh-wet'*]—cantering in a small tight circle, with the hind legs almost in the same spot; one of the basic movements, or "Schools on the Ground," used in the Spanish Riding School.

pituitary gland—secretes hormones influencing growth and metabolism.

pivot—to turn in place.

placed (see also **pinned**)—in racing, second place.

placenta [*pluh-sent'-uh*]—afterbirth; a vascular organ that surrounds the fetus during gestation and is connected to it by the umbilical cord; the fetus receives nourishment and excretes waste matter via this organ.

placental [*pluh-sent'-ul*]—of or pertaining to the placenta.

plantar—pertaining to the sole of the foot.

plantation saddle—see **saddle, English**

plater—see **farrier**

pleasure cart—see **cart**

pleural cavity [*plur'-ul*]—the body cavity containing the lungs and thorax.

pleuritis [*plur-eye'-tis*]—inflammation of the pleural lining of the lung.

plow rein (also "direct rein")—used to make the horse turn its head; rein applies pressure to the side to which the horse is asked to turn.

pinworms—intestinal parasites that cause irritation and tail rubbing.

pneumonia [*new-moan'-yuh*]—a disease of the lungs causing fluid accumulation within.

point rider—see **hilltopper**

points—1) the lower legs, mane, tail, and nose of the horse; 2) numbers accumulated in various equestrian events, for "high-point" score or award.

pole barn—barn built on poles that have been sunk into the soil.

pole bending—a western pattern that tests the horse's ability to make repetitive turns to the right and left while weaving in and out of poles, cones or barrels set in a line.

poleys—knee pads on an Australian saddle.

poll [*pole*]—the very top of the horse's head, between the ears; it is extremely sensitive.

poll guard—see **head bumper**

polo—a sporting game similar to hockey, played by teams on horseback.

polyestrus—a mare that cycles throughout the year.

polyuria—excessive urination.

pommel [*pah'-mul*]—the front portion of a saddle.

pony—1) (*n*) a breed of horse that will reach a maximum height of 14.2 hands (58 inches) at maturity; 2) (*n*) in racing, any horse or pony that heads the field or a starter from the paddock to the starting gate; 3) (*v*) to lead a horse while mounted on another horse ("*to pony*").

"popped a splint"—periostitis of the splint bone (see also **periostitis**).

"popped knee" (also "carpitis" "enlarged knee")—enlargement of the knee joint as a result of chip fracture, increased joint fluid, or arthritis.

port—the curved portion of the mouthpiece of a curb bit; the port concentrates the pressure on the bars of the mouth; the port can be either low (mild) or high (severe).

post—1) (*n*) starting point for a race; 2) (*v*) record a win.

post entry—in showing, an exhibitor that enters a class after the deadline.

post horn—the horn on a team roping saddle.

post position—in racing, the position of the stall in the starting gate.

post time—the time a race is scheduled to begin.

posterior—behind or after.

posting (also "posting at the trot")—the motion of rising to the trot; a forward and back motion on alternate beats at the trot.

postnatal—pertaining to the foal after birth.

postpartum—pertaining to the mare during the period following delivery of the foal.

potentiate [*poh-ten'-she-ate*]—to increase or multiply the effect of a drug or medication.

Potomac Horse Fever—a serious disease of horses that causes laminitis, fever, and diarrhea; immunization has reduced the death rate.

poultice [*pole'-tiss*]—a hot, moist mass applied to sore or inflamed area.

predispose—to make receptive ahead of time.

premature—a foal born between gestation days 300 and 325.

premium book (also "prize list" "entry book")—in showing, the advance information regarding classes, dates, entry deadlines, fees, etc.

prenatal—pertaining to the foal before birth.

prepotency [*pree-poh'-tent-see*]—term used to describe stallions that consistently reproduce their best traits or characteristics in their offspring.

pressure points—areas on the horse's head that are sensitive to the bridle and therefore useful for giving signals to it; included are the poll, corners of lips, bars of mouth, chin groove, tongue, roof of mouth, and nose.

private treaty—term used by stallion owner when a stud fee is not publicized.

prize list—see **premium book**

producer—term used for a productive mare.

professional trainer—a person whose vocation is training horses and for which that person is paid.

proficiency—expertise and skill in riding or training.

progenitor [*proh-jen'-ih-tur*]—term used for a productive stallion.

progeny [*prah'-ji-nee*]—offspring of either mare or stallion.

progesterone [*proh-jes'-ter-own*]—hormone produced by the corpus luteum that allows pregnancy to progress or causes the uterus to respond as if pregnant.

prognathism [*prog'-nuh-thih-zum*] (also "monkey mouth" "undershot jaw" "bulldog mouth")—mouth abnormality in which the lower jaw sticks out farther than the upper.

prognosis—the predicted outlook in a disease or condition.

prolactin [*proh-lak'-tin*]—the hormone that stimulates milk production.

Prostaglandin F2alpha (PGF2a)—the hormone generated by the uterus that affects the corpus luteum and causes it to degenerate.

prostaglandins [*prah'-stuh-glan-dins*]—substances released by the body in response to pain, injury, disease, or infection.

protest—1) (*v*) in showing, to lodge a formal complaint regarding judging scores, management, other exhibitors, etc.; 2) (*n*) a written formal complaint.

proud flesh—the scar tissue that builds up in excess at the site of a healing wound.

proximal—toward the body.

ptosis [*toe'-sis*]—a condition where the eyelids of the eye are slightly closed due to a nerve deficit.

pulled mane/tail—removing the longest hairs to give a neat, shorter appearance.

pulley rein—emergency rein for controlling a horse that gets its head down, bucks, or refuses to stop with ordinary rein control.

pumiced foot—see **dropped sole**

pure line—a strain that breeds true for certain characteristics.

purebred—a breed with consistently recognized characteristics maintained through generations of unmixed descent.

purpura hemorrhagica [*purr'-purr-uh hem-or-raj'-ih-kuh*]—a complication of strangles where blood vessels become inflamed and cause swelling of the head and limbs.

purse—in racing, the term for the prize money or winnings.

purulent [*pure'-you-lent*]—containing or forming pus.

pus—the liquid matter produced in infections, consisting of bacteria, white blood cells, serum.

pustule [*puhs'-chewl*]—an elevation of the skin containing pus.

"put down"—see **euthanize**

pyramidal disease (also "buttress foot")—a foot deformity caused by torn fibers of the digital extensor tendon; a bulge develops and the foot contracts.

Q

qualifier—a show, race, or trial that earns qualifying points toward a larger show, such as a national or international show.

qualitative—pertaining to quality; controlled by one element.

quantitative—pertaining to quantity; controlled by many different elements.

quarantine—isolation; official removal of diseased animals to a restricted area for treatment or observation.

quarter—1) on the foot, the mid-section between the heel and toe; 2) in some breeds, the area more commonly called the haunch.

quarterboot—see **boots**

quarter crack—hoof defect where side of hoof is split from the ground to the coronary band; if deep enough, this can cause severe lameness.

quick—an injury of the foot caused by a nail driven through the hoof into the sensitive tissue, drawing blood and precipitating infection.

"quick-release knot" (also "slip knot")—a knot tied in such a way that it will hold the horse under normal circumstances, but can be jerked loose in a panic situation.

quiescent [*kwy-eh'-sent*]—quiet or resting.

quinella—in racing, when the first and second horses must be picked in either order.

quirt—a riding aid made of braided rawhide with leather lashes at the tip.

quittor (also "lateral cartilage necrosis")—destruction of tissue due to a puncture wound above the coronary band.

R

RMS—see **Repetitive Motion Syndrome**

RNA—1) *ribonucleic acid*, one of the two nucleic acids involved in the transmission of genetic material; 2) in a sale or auction, abbreviation for "Reserve Not Attained."

race starter—one who supervises the loading of horses into the starting gate and then starts the race.

racing secretary—one who arranges racing and stabling activities at a racetrack.

racing silks—see **silks**

racing sulky—a light two-wheeled vehicle used in harness racing.

rack (also "singlefoot")—an exaggerated, 4-beat very fast walk where each foot hits the ground separately at equal intervals; the horse has only one foot on the ground at any time during this gait.

racking horse—common term for a horse that has been trained to perform the rack.

"rack on"—in showing, the judges' direction for exhibitors to show their racking horses to the fullest.

radiographs—x-rays.

rail (also "fence")—term for the barrier around the outside of an enclosed arena, or the railing around the infield of a racetrack.

"railroad tracks"—in reining, the descriptive term for the skid marks left by the horse's hind feet in a sliding stop.

rain rot (also "pasture rot" or "rain scald")—a bacterial condition in horses that is exacerbated by moisture on abraded or damaged skin.

rain scald—see **rain rot**

ranch saddle—see **saddle, western; cowhand**

random mating—selection of a mate without regard to genotype.

rapport [*ra-pore'*]—harmony, or agreement.

reata [*ree-ah'-tuh*]—a rope made of rawhide.

reabsorbed—see **resorbed**

receptors—nerve endings that are capable of receiving stimulation.

recessive—not dominant.

recipient mare—the mare in which an embryo transfer is implanted.

record—a documented history of a horse's breeding and/or show record.

rectum—the last portion of the large intestine.

refinement—having elegance of build and conformation; having fine, delicate features.

refractory—not yielding to treatment; resistant.

refusal (also "run-out" "balk")—1) a horse stopping in front of a fence; not jumping over it; 2) in racing, a horse not breaking from the starting gate.

registration—the official listing and documentation, in a particular registry, of a horse of that breed.

registry—an organization that oversees and conducts the registration of purebred livestock.

regression—going back or going away; becoming less.

rein board—a driving apparatus for practicing the use of reins.

reining—a western competitive event where the horses are required to perform a series of patterns and maneuvers on which points are scored.

reins (also "lines")—the leather lines attached to the bridle with which the rider or driver directs the horse.

remuda [*reh-mew'-duh*] (also "cavvy")—a band of working saddle horses.

Repetitive Motion Syndrome (RMS)—disabling soreness in certain muscle and joint groups caused by repeated overwork of those areas.

reserve—1) a minimum price placed by the consignor on a horse for sale at auction; 2) second place to Champion.

resistance—rejection of the rider's aids; includes throwing the head in the air, opening the mouth, crossing the jaw, or hollowing the back.

resolution—(*n*) clearing up, complete recovery.

resolve—(*v*) to clear up, recover.

resorbed (also "reabsorbed")—absorption of an early embryo into the mare's system.

respiration—breathing.

respiratory—relating to the lungs and chest.

retained cap—when a temporary tooth does not release from the gum.

retained placenta—afterbirth that is not expelled within 6 hours after foaling.

retention—the process or condition of keeping fluids or solids within the body, rather than excreting them.

reverse—in the arena or ring, turning the horse off the rail toward the center of the ring, then returning to the rail going in the other direction.

Reynard—see **Charley**

rhinitis [*rye-nye'-tus*]—inflammation of the nasal mucous membrane.

Rhino—see **Rhinopneumonitis**

rhino virus—the virus causing Rhinopneumonitis.

Rhinopneumonitis [*rye-no-new-men-eye'-tus*] (also "rhino")—a highly-contagious disease causing abortion in pregnant mares or mild upper respiratory infection in young horses.

ridgeling [*ridj'-ling*] (also "rig")—term for a horse that is either a cryptorchid or monorchid.

riding habit (also "hunt habit")—English-style riding attire consisting of breeches, jacket, shirt, stock tie, hunt cap, and high boots.

"riding on contact"—rider maintains a gentle feel on the horse's mouth at all times; reins are stretched lightly, but not pulling.

rig—see **ridgeling**

rigging—straps on a western saddle that connect the cinch and tree.

ring—common term for the area where a horse is worked or where classes are held in a horse show.

ring steward—in showing, the person who acts as a liaison between exhibitors and judges.

ringbone—form of arthritis settling in pastern bones; can cause progessive lameness.

ringworm—a highly-contagious fungal infection affecting the skin; there are no worms involved.

roach back—a conformation defect where the horse's back is convex.

roaching—(see also **hogging**)—clipping the mane completely down the neck, except where some of the hairs are left longer at the top of the withers.

road cart—see **cart**

road trot—an extended trot that is faster than a normal trot and covers more space in each stride.

roadster—see **cart**

roadster class (also "sulky class")—a driving class where speed is the object; horses use three different speeds of the trot: jog trot, road trot, and drive-on trot; drivers wear racing silks.

roan—a haircoat that is a combination of white or silver and colored hairs (except grey and true white); **bay r.**—a haircoat that is a combination of dark brown and white hairs; **blue r.**—a haircoat that is a combination of black and white hairs; **strawberry r.**—a haircoat that is a combination of white and chestnut hairs.

roaning—the genetically-produced pattern of silver hairs mixed into the main body coat color.

roaring (also "laryngeal paresis")—a loud whistling, raspy noise made by a horse during exercise; caused by paralysis of certain of the laryngeal muscles.

rodeo—an event where cowboys gather to compete in tests of skill such as calf roping, bronc riding, etc.

rogue—a bad-tempered, nasty horse.

rollback—in reining, a 180-degree reversal of forward motion. The horse runs to a stop, turns the shoulders back to the opposite direction over the hocks, and departs in a canter, all in one continuous motion.

rolling—when a horse lies down and rolls back and forth, either for pleasure, or due to pain.

romal (also "California rein") [*row-mahl'*]—leather strap attached to a ring holding the rider ends of both reins.

roman nose—having a hump in the center.

rope horse—see **calf horse**

rosaderos—see **fenders**

rosettes—1) decorations on dressage and driving bridles; 2) award ribbons.

rotavirus—a virus that causes severe diarrhea in horses.

roughage—feed that consists of any combination of hay, pasture or pelleted hay; needed by horses for proper digestion.

round pen (also "round corral" "stallion pen")—a circular exercise corral.

roundworms—see **ascarids**

rowels—on western spurs, a wheel with blunt points.

rubbernecking—the term used to describe a horse that bends the neck when asked to turn, instead of following the bit pressure.

rubefacient [*roo-beh-fah'-shent*]—a topical analgesic that promotes heat and increased blood flow to an area.

rug—1) (also "blanket") a warm blanket for horses; (see also **New Zealand rug**) 2) (also "lap robe")— see **driving apron**.

run—see **gallop**

run-down boot—see **boots; sesamoid**

run-in shed—a shelter in the pasture or field that is usually 3-sided and provides a place to get out of the sun, rain, or snow.

running martingale—see **martingale**

running strides—too fast and with quick, unbalanced strides.

running walk—a natural gait of the Tennessee Walking Horse in which three feet are on the ground and one foot is in the air.

un-off at the croup—see **run-off croup**

un-off croup (also "run-off at the croup")—a sloping croup.

un-out (also "refusal")—in jumping, when a horse approaches the fence, then turns and runs away from it to avoid jumping.

upture—a split or tear in an organ or vessel, usually caused by pressure.

usset—a yellowish or reddish brown color used on saddlery and harness.

 S

acking—grooming technique in which a piece of burlap (feed sacking) or coarse toweling is lightly slapped against the horse all over its body to bring up the natural oils and make the haircoat shine.

addle—in driving, the portion of harness that lies on the horse's back where a rider would sit.

addle, English—1) term for any of various styles of saddle used for huntseat, dressage, eventing, jumping, racing, or saddleseat riding; **Australian s.**-saddle designed with a deep seat, knee pads known as "poleys," and wide leg leathers; **close-contact jumping s.** (also "flat jumping" "French" "Olympic" "Hermes")-a flat saddle with minimum bulk under the legs and a low cantle; **endurance s.**-see "endurance saddle"; **plantation s.**-a well-padded flat saddle with a supportive cantle, used for long days on horseback; **show s.**-an English saddle favored in saddleseat riding, where the rider sits back on a very flat seat to show off the horse's animated gaits; **side s.**-an English saddle having a large flat seat and two pommels with horns called "heads" that hold the legs in place; also known as a "hunting sidesaddle"; originally designed for ladies

addle, western—term for any of various styles of saddle used for working horses, western events, or western riding; **balanced ride s.**-a forward seat type saddle with a flat seat and stirrup leathers on a swivel; **barrel racing s.**-a lightweight saddle with a high cantle and tall horn; **calf-roping s.**-a roping saddle with a short horn; **cowhand s.** (also "ranch" "buckaroo")-a plain saddle with an upright seat, high pommel and horn; **deep seat equitation s.**-used for showing in equitation; **Peruvian s.** (also "montura")-saddle with high pommel and cantle; developed for Peruvian Pasos; **pleasure western s.**-a saddle with a deep seat and small horn; **stock s.**-a western saddle with a horn at the pommel and a high cantle; used originally for working cattle on the range; **team roping s.**-saddle with a tall, vertical horn called a "post horn."

addle blanket—a sturdy, soft covering that protects the horse's back under the saddle.

addle galls—see **saddle sores**

addle horse—see **saddle-type**

addle mark—a mark behind the withers usually caused by poor saddle fit.

addle pad—see **pad**

addle seat—English style riding where the rider sits back in the saddle to enhance the display of foreleg action in saddle horses.

addle sores (also "saddle galls")—abrasions caused by the saddle rubbing against a hair coat that is not clean.

addle tree—the framework of a saddle.

addle-type (also "saddle horse")—horses that are showy, smooth, and pleasant to ride with brilliant gaits and a refined appearance; usually have small heads carried high, long neck, flat back and croup, and high tail set; developed for precision of gait.

addle up—the act of putting a saddle on a horse.

aliva—the exudate of the mucous membrane within the mouth.

anctioned (also "approved")—endorsed, as in "AHSA sanctioned show."

and crack—see **heel crack**

arcoid—skin tumor.

savage—*(v)* term for a horse biting viciously.

sawbuck (also "crossbuck")—common pack saddle consisting of 2 pair of crosspieces called "bucks" that fit over the horse's withers; they are then fitted onto the saddle tree and secured with two cinches.

scabbard—a rifle holder on a western saddle.

scabs—hard crusts composed of debris, pus, and serum that form over a wound.

scar tissue—tough, white or grey, non-elastic tissue that forms over an area of injury.

sclera [*sklair'-uh*]—the white of the eye.

schooling—training a horse; **s. show**—a competition that is used for practice; **s. horse**—a calm, very well-trained horse that is suitable and safe for beginning riders.

Scotch hobble—see **hobbles**

scours—normal bout of diarrhea in a foal at the time its dam comes into the foal heat.

scratch—*(v)* remove a horse from a class or race, usually due to health considerations.

scratches (also "mud cracks")—a painful condition of the posterior pastern caused by mud and hair that is constantly wet.

scrotum—the sac containing the testicles.

scurf—dry skin; dandruff.

season—see **stallion season; "in season"**

seat—the correct position of the body while riding any discipline.

secondary—referring to a condition that occurs as a result of a primary or original condition.

secretion—the fluid or mucus that is produced and released by a gland or tissue.

seeding—referring to re-infecting the ground with parasite eggs.

seedy toe—a condition, resulting from founder, where the sensitive and insensitive laminae separate at the white line.

selection—the process of upgrading a herd of animals; see also **artificial s., natural s.**

selenium—an element found in soil that is required by growing horses.

senior—in combined training, an exhibitor who has reached either the age of 19 or 22, depending upon the competition divisions.

sensitive frog—the portion of the hoof that nourishes the horny frog.

sensitive laminae—leaf-like structures that lie between the hoofwall and the coffin bone, which in conjunction with other structures, suspend and support nearly the entire weight of the horse during the support phase of a stride.

sensitive sole—the portion of the sole that covers the bottom of the coffin bone and nourishes the cells that produce the horny sole.

semen—thick white fluid containing sperm.

septic—having an infectious nature.

septicemia [*sehp-tih-see'-mee-uh*] (also "blood poisoning")—a serious condition caused by bacteria in the bloodstream.

septum—the wall between two cavities.

serous [*sear'-us*]—thin and watery; containing serum.

serpentine—a snake-like riding pattern using half circles back and forth from right to left.

serum—thin watery animal fluid, especially in the blood.

sesamoid bone [*seh'-suh-moyd*]—pyramid-shaped bone at the back of the fetlock joint next to the cannon bone; this bone acts as a fulcrum.

sesamoid boot—see **boots**

settle (also "conceive")—become pregnant.

sex chromosomes—those that determine the sex of an organism.

shackles—used to train gaited horses for high action; boots fit over the shod foot and are held in place on the saddle or body roller.

shadow roll—in racing, a thick roll that is placed on the noseband of the bridle to keep the horse from seeing shadows that might spook it.

shafts—the long poles extending out from a driving vehicle, to which the harness is attached.

shanks—see **cheeks**

sheath—the protective covering of the penis.

shedding blade—a blade with short teeth that removes loose hair from the coat.

shedrow—see **stable**

sheet—a covering, designed like a blanket, but made of lighter weight material; **anti-sweat s.**—a covering made of open weave or mesh.

sheet cotton—pressed cotton in thin sheets that is used under leg wraps.

shin buck—see **shin splints**

shin splints (also "shin buck")—irritated or torn periosteum on the front of the cannon bone.

shipping boot—see **boots**

shivering—nervous disorder in the horse that is characterized by overflexion of the hocks, inability to lower the foot to the ground, and tremors.

shod—wearing horseshoes.

shoer—see **farrier**

short cycle—to bring a mare back to receptivity sooner than the 21 days standard; this is done by administering a timed dose of PGF2a.

short head—British term for "win by a nose."

show—1) (*n*) an equestrian event where horses are exhibited in various types of activities; 2) (*v*) in showing, to exhibit or present a horse to the judges and spectators; 3) in racing, the third position at the finish line.

show saddle—see **saddle, English**

showmanship—a type of class that exhibits the skill with which an exhibitor presents his or her horse.

shy—to suddenly leap or move to one side or the other, sometimes even rearing; usually in response to something that is perceived as threatening.

shying—quick, unpredictable movements by a horse that has become frightened or "spooked."

siblings—brothers and sisters.

"sickle hocks"—a conformation fault where the hind feet are in front of the hock.

sidebone—condition causing the collateral cartilage of the hoof to turn into bone.

sidechecks—leather strips on either side of the bridle of a harness; used for leverage and to set the head.

sidepass (also "side step")—a maneuver where the horse steps sideways by crossing over the front and hind feet at the same time.

sidepull—a western noseband fitted with a curb strap.

side reins—used to teach a horse to set his head; attached to the bridle at one end and the saddle or harness surcingle at the other.

sidesaddle—see **saddle, English**

side step—see **sidepass**

silent heat—ovulation without the behavioral signs of heat.

silks (also "racing silks")—in racing, a shirt that displays the farm colors or the post position.

simple course—a course of fences consisting of two or more lines of fences with turns.

singlefoot—see **rack**

singletree—a bar hung between the shafts of a carriage, to which the ends of the traces are attached.

sinusitis—inflammation of the sinuses, causing swelling, pain, and discharge.

sire—(*n*) father.

sired by—(*v*) fathered.

"sitting the trot" (also "sitting trot")—staying in contact with the horse through each movement of the trot; not posting.

sitting trot—see **"sitting the trot"**

skewbald—a parti-color horse with a haircoat in a non-white color patterned with white.

skid boot—see **boots**

skirt—on a saddle, the flap of leather covering the stirrup bar attachment on each side.

slab-sided—conformation fault characterized by a barrel that is not completely round; the horse is frequently narrow-chested.

sleeping sickness—see **equine encephalomyelitis**

slicker—riding raingear with a wide skirt that covers the entire saddle.

sliding boot—see **boots**

sliding ear headstall—a western headstall with a loop over the ear rather than a browband.

sliding stop—in cutting and reining, a stop where the horse drops down on its haunches and plants its feet firmly while sliding to a stop, leaving "railroad tracks" in the footing behind.

slip knot—see **quick-release knot**

slipped—in breeding, a term meaning spontaneous abortion; ("slipped her foal").

slough [*sluhf*]—shedding of dead tissue.

slow gait—in gaited horses, a rack that is slower than a regular rack.

slow track—in racing, a track that is wet from the surface down into the base.

smegma—oily secretions that accumulate under the sheath of the stallion's penis.

snaffle bit—the most common jointed direct pressure bit used for lateral control; usually mild and used for green horses or beginning riders.

snip—a single white mark near the nostril.

"snots"—term for thick mucus discharge that is a symptom of rhinopneumonitis in foals.

sock (also "anklet")—white color marking that extends from the hoof to the fetlock joint.

sole—the bottom of the hoof.

"soring"—the application of highly-irritating oil of mustard to the pasterns, causing the horse to exaggerate the lift of the legs.

sorrel [*sore'-ul*]—a western term for chestnut color.

sound—healthy and usable.

soundness—quality of physical fitness.

sow mouth—see **brachygnathism**

spade bit—a severe curb bit with a very high port, resembling a spoon, that touches the roof of the horse's mouth.

species—a distinct kind or type of organism.

species hybridization—the mating of members of different species.

sperm—the male sex cell which carries the genetic information.

spermatozoa [*sper-ma-tuh-zoe'-uh*]—the male sex cell, composed of a head, which carries the genetic information, and tail (flagellum) which is used for propulsion.

spermicidal—having the ability to destroy sperm.

spike or spike-nose cavesson—see **cavesson**

spin—in reining, a 360-degree turn, executed with the inside hind leg remaining stationary.

splay footed—see **toe out**

splint—a bony growth between the cannon bone and the splint bone, resulting from excessive concussion.

splint bones—bones on both sides and back of the cannon bone; the upper ends are part of the bearing surface of the knee.

split class—in showing, when a class has a large number of entries and management deems it necessary to split the class into two sections; each section competes and the winners of the two sections compete for the final placings.

split heat—term for double ovulation within the space of a few days.

split pastern—a broken pastern bone caused by strain on the tendons as a result of pasterns that are too long.

spontaneous—having no apparent external cause or influence; happening as a result of internal energy.

spook—term for the unpredictable actions of a horse that becomes frightened by something, either real or imaginary.

sprain—a severe strain; pulled or stretched muscle or ligament.

spraddling out—see **traveling wide**

spread fence—built with some width, the front being lower than the back.

sprint—*(n)* a race that is less than one mile.

sprinter—in racing, a horse that performs best over short distances at speed.

spur (also "gad")—*(n)* a riding aid that is attached to the rider's boot; made of metal or very hard synthetic materials; used for urging the horse forward; *(v)* to urge or kick the horse to move, using spurs.

squamous cell [*skway'-mus*]—flat cell having the appearance of a scale.

stable (also "barn" "livery" "shedrow")—facility that is designed to house horses.

stable livery—see **undress livery**

staff—in hunting, the huntsman and whippers-in.

stag—a male horse that has been gelded after being used for a breeding stallion.

stagnant—standing water that has become brackish and sour.

stake horse—1) in racing, a horse that runs in stake races; 2) see **"big lick horse"**

stake out—to tie a horse on a long line attached to a stake driven into the ground.

stake race—see **stakes**

stakes (also "stake race")—in racing, a race where the owner pays a fee to run a horse.

stall—a barn enclosure for holding horses; **box s.**—a roomy living stall of approximately 12 x 12 feet; **foaling s.**—a large stall of appoximately 14 x 14 to 16 x 16 feet, used for housing expectant mares for delivery; **standing s.**—a stall of approximately 8' to 10' by 5' to 6' for keeping a horse for short periods of time; the size prohibits lying down or turning around; **straight s.**—a two-sided stall with a manger at the front, but no door; horse is tied; a short-term enclosure.

stall vices—bad habits acquired by horses that become bored standing in a stall all day and night.

stall walker—a horse that constantly paces its stall and doesn't rest.

stallion—an adult male horse capable of producing offspring.

stallion condom—a rubber recepticle used for collecting semen.

stallion pen—see **round pen**

stallion ring—a ring made of rubber or plastic that is slipped over the penis to discourage erection.

stallion season—the right to breed a mare to a stallion during one breeding season.

stallion share—lifetime breeding rights to a stallion, at one mare per season per share.

stallion syndicate—an investment group that owns shares in a stallion.

stamina—endurance; resistance to fatigue, hardship, etc.

stand—*(v)* to make a stallion available for breeding.

standing bandages—leg wraps applied when a horse will not be moving around; these keep the legs from swelling due to accumulated fluid.

standing martingale—see **martingale**

standing over—leg conformation in which the lower leg is behind the vertical.

standing under—poor leg conformation where the lower leg is in front of the vertical.

star—a white face marking on the forehead.

stay apparatus—a set of ligaments and tendons in the hind legs that allow the horse to sleep and relax in the standing position; this system also supports the fetlock, diminishes concussion, and prevents excessive flexion of the fetlock, pastern, and coffin joints.

stayer—in racing, a horse who performs best over a longer distance.

steeplechase (also "chase")—a race where horses jump a series of obstacles on the course.

steer wrestling—see **bulldogging**

stenosis—stricture or narrowing.

sterile—1) infertile, barren; 2) clean, without microorganisms.

stethoscope—an instrument used for listening to internal sounds.

steward—see **ring steward**

stick—1) in racing, a jockey's whip; 2) the measuring stick for horse heights.

stickers—see **calks**

stifle [*sty'-ful*]—the knee-like joint above the hock.

stifled—affliction where the stifle joint locks as a result of poor conformation and loose ligaments; can be corrected by surgery.

stillbirth—birth of a dead fetus.

stimulation—to excite or arouse to activity.

stirrup—the foothold on a saddle; English stirrups are made of metal and are removable; western stirrups are made of wood covered in leather.

stock—1) a restraining chute; 2) short term for livestock.

stock pin—a safety-type pin used to secure a stock tie in English or hunt riding attire.

stock saddle—see **saddle, western**

stock tie—a long tie wrapped about the neck and secured with a stock pin.

stock-type—horses with large, well-developed hindquarters and strong forearm muscles; compact, short-coupled, and agile for quick starts and stops; not usually tall or long-legged; developed for precision of speed.

stocked up—term for swelling in the lower legs of a horse.

stocking—white leg marking that extends to the knee or hock.

strain—a mild injury to muscle or ligament.

strangles (also "distemper")—an infectious and highly contagious disease, occurring most commonly in young horses; high temperature, thick nasal discharge and swelling of lymphatic glands of the head, which eventually abscess.

strapgoods—term for leather straps, lines, reins, traces, chin straps, etc.

stratum tectorum—a thin layer of horny scales that gives the hoof its glossy appearance and protects against evaporation.

Streptococcus equi—the bacteria that cause strangles.

stride—1) way of going; **flat s.**—little or no suspension in the sequence; **irregular s.**—irregular rhythm of the pace; **running s.**—too fast and with quick, unbalanced strides; **uneven s.**—strides of different lengths; **unlevel s.**—unequal strides with both hindlegs or both forelegs; 2) distance between successive imprints of the same hoof.

strike—1) to aim a blow or kick with the front leg; 2) in hunting, to find a fox.

stringhalt—an exaggerated flexion of the horse's hock while the horse is in motion.

strip—a narrow band of white that extends the length of the face.

strip clip—removing only the hair on the underside of the jaw, down the jugular vein, across the chest, and on the underside of the belly.

stripping stalls—the complete removal of all bedding and replacement with clean, fresh bedding; usually done 3-4 times per month, depending on preference and other factors such as weather.

strongyles (also "bloodworms")—life-threatening intestinal parasites of horses.

stud—1) a stallion used for breeding; 2) term for a horse-breeding farm.

stud book—a registry and geneology record maintained by a breed registry.

stud fee—the charge for breeding to a stallion.

"stump sucking"—see **cribbing**

stunted—not reaching full size or shape at maturity.

subchondral cyst—see **osteochondritis**

subcutaneous [*sub-kew-tay'-nee-us*]—beneath the skin.

suckling—an unweaned foal.

suffocation—death from lack of oxygen.

sulky—a two-wheeled driving vehicle used for racing.

sulky class—see **roadster class**

superficial—on the surface, not deep.

supple—relaxed and flexible; able to bend and turn with ease.

supplement—in nutrition, any one or combination of ingredients added to the horse's regular feed.

supplemental—in addition to.

surcingle [*sir'-sing-gul*] (also "lunge roller" "body roller")—a wide strap attached to a pad and buckled into place; used for securing blankets and coolers or as part of a bitting harness.

surrey—a 4-wheeled light carriage having two seats and a flat top.

susceptible—vulnerable; easily attacked or compromised.

suspensory—holding a bone or limb in a suspended manner.

suspensory ligament—the major ligament in the back of the cannon bone.

suturing—the closure of an open wound by sewing it shut.

swamp fever—see **Equine Infectious Anemia**

sway back (also "hollow back")—sign of weak conformation through the spine, being concave just behind the withers and usually accompanied by low-slung belly, often seen in old horses, especially broodmares.

sweat—1) a topical analgesic that causes moisture to be drawn out of the underlying tissues and to accumulate on the skin; 2) a wrap used to reduce the thickness or bulk by sweating.

sweat scraper—a dull metal or plastic strip used for whisking away excess foamy sweat or excess water after a bath.

sweeney—atrophy of the shoulder muscles as a result of strain- or trauma-induced paralysis of the suprascapular (above the scapula) nerve.

sweet feed—mixed grain feed that contains molasses.

swing time—during the gallop, the time that each leg spends in the airborne phase of the stride.

swipe—see **groom**

symmetrical—evenly shaped.

systemic—within the entire body system, rather than particular parts.

 T

tack—all the leather equipment used for training or using a horse, such as halter, harness, bridle, etc.

tack room—an area in a barn or stable where equipment is kept.

tack shop—a store specializing in horse equipment and supplies.

tack stall—in showing, a stall that is used as a place to keep tack and supplies.

tack trunk—a portable container for carrying tack and supplies to and from shows; can be a permanent part of the tack room also.

tacking up—saddling and bridling a horse to go riding.

tactile—by touch.

tail female line—the descending or ascending line of dams from a particular mare.

tail male line—the descending or ascending line of sires from a particular stallion.

tail rope—a rope attached to the tail with a half-hitch and then tied to the neck or harness.

tail wrap—material used to wrap a mare's tail for protection and cleanliness during breeding, examination, or foaling; or to keep a braided show tail intact.

tail wringing—a habit or vice in which the horse wrings its tail around in a circle; this can sometimes indicate displeasure at being asked to perform.

Tally-Ho—in foxhunting, the cheer or cry used when the fox is spotted.

Tally-Ho back—in foxhunting, to turn back the fox when it comes out.

tandem hitch—in driving, a pair of horses hitched one in front of the other.

tapadero—a leather hood over the front and top of a western stirrup.

tattoo—a permanent mark on the inside of the upper lip; used for identification of horses, especially in racing.

teamster—name of the person who manages a team of work horses.

teaser—a male horse or pony used to detect heat in a mare.

teasing—the procedure for evaluating a mare's proximity to heat or readiness to be bred.

teat—nipple.

temperament (also "disposition")—nature, frame of mind.

temporomandibular joint [*tem-pore-oh-man-dih'-bew-lur*]—the jaw hinge.

tendinitis—inflammation of any tendon; (also see **bowed tendons**)

tendon—a fibrous cord of connective tissue that attaches muscle to bone or other structures.

tendon boot—see **boots**

tendon sheath—the thin membrane covering the outside of a tendon.

term(also "full term")—describes a pregnancy that has progressed for the full amount of time required for normal birth.

terrets—metal rings on a harness through which the reins pass.

test jump—to allow a teaser to mount the mare to see her reaction before allowing the breeding stallion to mount.

testis—male gonad.

testicles—the structure containing the male gonads.

Tetanus (also "lockjaw")—an infectious, often fatal disease caused by a micro-organism living in the soil; usually enters the body through wounds, especially of the foot.

tetany—spasms of a muscle that cause it to become rigid.

tether—(*v*) to tie a horse when not using it; (*n*) a tie-rope or lunge-line.

"tethered work"—see **lunging**

Texas gate—in jumping, a gate made of barbed wire.

therapeutic—beneficial; pertaining to treatment.

thimbles—the leather pouches into which the ends of the cart shafts are inserted; these act as "brakes" for the shafts, keeping the vehicle from running into the horse.

thoracolumbar [*thor-uh-ko-lum'-bar*]—pertaining to the full back.

throatlatch (also "throatlash" "throttle")—1) the area where the lower jaw meets the throat portion of the neck; 2) the part of a bridle that buckles under the jaw (at the throatlatch).

throttle—see **throatlatch**

throughpin—distention of the sheath of the deep flexor tendon at the hock, showing up as a visible bulge on the leg.

thrush—inflammation of the frog of the foot, characterized by a foul-smelling discharge; caused by unclean, damp bedding or pasture, and lack of proper hoof cleaning.

thruster—in hunting, an inexperienced rider who makes a pest of himself by larking over fences or pushing the hounds.

tie-down—1) a western version of the standing martingale that attaches to a bosal or noseband; 2) on harness, the strap that secures the shaft in the tugs.

tied—see **pinned**

"tied in behind the knee" (also *"tied in below the knee"*)—conformation deviation in the leg where the flexor tendons appear to be too close to the cannon bone, just below the knee.

"tied-on" (also "tied-on hard & fast")—in calf roping, when the rope is tied to the saddle horn.

tightener—a topical analgesic that aids in the removal of fluid from tendon sheaths and joint capsules.

tilting head—nose is raised and turned to either side, making the head slant to either side.

timothy—grass hay.

tincture [*tink'-shur*]—a medicinal substance that has been lightened with alcohol or a water/alcohol combination.

tobiano [*toe-bee-ah'-no*]—a parti-color horse with four white legs, a solid color body and other white markings.

toe in (also "pigeon-toed" "toe narrow")—a conformation fault where the feet point inwards.

toe narrow—see **toe in**

toe out (also "splay-footed" "toe wide")—a conformation fault where the feet point outwards.

toe wide—see **toe out**

Tom Thumb—see **jointed curb**

tongue strap (also "tongue tie")—a strip of cloth used to stabilize a horse's tongue so that it will not choke while exerting itself, or be able to slide the tongue up over the bit, thereby becoming uncontrollable.

tongue tie—see **tongue strap**

topical—applied to the surface of the skin.

topline—1) the outline of the horse from the poll to the croup; 2) the upper ancestral line (sire's side) in a pedigree diagram.

torsion [*tor'-shun*]—being twisted, especially the intestine.

toxicity—having the capacity to poison.

toxicosis—poisoning.

toxin—a poison.

toxoid—a toxin that has been made nonpoisonous without impairing its ability to stimulate antibody formation.

trace clip—a partial body clip that covers the throat, neck, chest, underbelly, and up the sides to where the traces of harness would lie if the horse were hitched.

traces—the lines attached to the breastplate that run back and attach to the driving vehicle.

trachea [*tray'-kee-uh*] (also "windpipe")—the airway from the nasal passages to the lungs.

tracheal [*tray'-kee-ul*]—of or pertaining to the trachea.

tracheotomy [*tray-kee-ah'-tuh-mee*]—a surgical procedure where an opening is made into the trachea from the outside of the body, in order to relieve obstruction of breathing.

tracking—term for the degree of straightness in where a horse places its feet during a gait.

tractable—easily managed or handled.

tractability—managability.

traction—adhesive friction used for movement, as of the horse's foot on the ground.

trail course designer—see **trail engineer**

trail engineer—one who designs and supervises the construction of riding trails.

trail ride—an event staged for either pleasure or competition, in which horses are ridden out in the natural environment.

trailer—1) (also "horse box" "horse van") a vehicle for transporting horses; 2) an extension of the heel of a horseshoe.

trailer tie—a short tie-rope that keeps the horse's head up and facing the front of the trailer.

trainer (also "handler")—an individual who trains horses for other people.

trainability—physical and mental parameters that affect a horse's ability to be trained.

training whip (also "dressage whip")—a long, thin whip measuring 36-39 inches, used to tap the horse's side just behind the rider's leg without taking hands off the reins.

trait—a distinguishing quality or characteristic.

transition—to change from one gait to another, or change in speed during a gait.

trauma [*traw'-muh*]—bodily injury, wound, or shock.

traveling wide (also "spraddling out")—at the walk or trot, the distance between the hocks is greater than the imaginary lines drawn through the centers of the legs.

treble—a jump composed of 3 fences close together.

tremors—trembling of the limbs, caused by muscle spasm.

trifecta (also "triple") ["*triactor*" *in Canada*]—placing a bet on the first three finishers in exact order.

trimester—one-third of a full-term pregnancy.

triple—see **trifecta**

triple bar—a jump coposed of 3 rails of different heights in stair-step fashion.

trochanteric bursitis [*trow-kan-tare'-ik ber-sigh'-tis*] (also "whirlbone lameness")—an inflammation of the area between the greater trochanter and middle gluteal muscle tendon, usually caused by excessive work in a circle or turning.

trot—a gait that uses a two-beat rhythm; **collected t.**—a pleasure class gait, steady and well-cadenced; **"drive-on" t.**-a roadster driving gait that is the fastest trot; **extended t.**—steady, but a bit faster than a collected trot, and covering more ground; **road t.**—a fast, very extended driving gait; **working t.**—a brisk, snappy, animated and showy trot with long strides.

trotting poles—see **cavaletti**

tub cart—see **governess cart**

tube—*(v)* insertion of a naso-gastric tube into the horse's nostrils and down into the stomach for administering medication.

tugs—heavy leather rings or straps hung from a harness backpad which carry the shafts of a one-horse vehicle.

tumor—a new growth of tissue that is independent of its surrounding environment and has no function

"tuned up"—term for a horse that has been worked or warmed up slightly to make i alert and ready to respond.

turn out—*(v)* to put horses out to pasture when not being used.

turnout—*(n)* the area in which horses are kept when not in the barn.

tushes—teeth found only on male horses.

twitch—a device used to restrain an unmanageable horse so that procedures such as clipping, vaccinations, or reproductive examinations can be performed; the device is used on the muzzle, producing a calming effect; **humane t.** (also "nose-clamp")—a light aluminum clamp-like device; **hand t.**—using the hand to twist the muzzle to produce the same effect.

two-minute rule—in showing, a rule stating that if an exhibitor has not entered the arena or ring within two minutes of the time the class is called, the gate will be closed and the exhibitor is disqualified from the class.

"tying up"—common term for acute *rhabdomyolysis*-a form of muscle cramps that affects horses and can be mild to severe.

type—1) built well or having a particular talent to do a particular job, regardless of breed (i.e., hunter type horse); 2) having specific characteristics that emphasize or typify a breed.

 U

udder—the mammary gland of the mare; also called the "bag."

ulcerated—tissue having an open sore.

ultrasound—ultrasonic waves used in diagnosis or pregnancy detection; sound waves at a very high frequency bounce against the fetus and then back to the monitor, forming a picture on the screen.

umbilical hernia—a condition in which the intestines protrude through the abdominal wall, in the area of the navel; commonly seen in foals.

umbilicus [*um-bih'-lih-kus*]—the belly button or navel through which a fetus absorbs its nourishment and discards its waste during gestation.

Uncle Remus—see **Charley**

"under harness" (also "in harness")—being worked in harness; driven.

"under saddle"—being worked with saddle and bridle; ridden.

underline—the line from the attachment of the elbow along the belly to the attachmen of the hind leg.

undershot jaw—see **prognathism**

undress livery (also "stable livery")—in driving, the informal working uniform of groom or coachman.

uneven strides—strides of different lengths.

unicorn hitch—in driving, a team of three horses with two hitched side by side and the third in front of the pair.

unilateral—on one side.

unlevel strides—unequal strides with both hindlegs or both forelegs.

unsound—a term for a horse that is not physically fit for the intended use.

unthrifty—in poor condition.

untried—1) in racing, a horse that has not been raced or timed for speed; 2) in breeding, a stallion that has not been bred.

"upside down neck"—see **ewe neck**

upward patella fixation—a painful condition where the back leg locks up at the stifle and will not bend; seen in young, fast-growing horses.

urethra [*you-ree'-thruh*]—the canal through which urine is excreted.

urethral [*you-ree'-thrul*]—of or pertaining to the urethra.

urinary incontinence—the condition of being unable to control urination.

uterus (also "wethers" "womb")—the reproductive organ in the mare where an embryo/fetus develops.

uveitis [*you-vee-eye'-tus*]—see **periodic ophthalmia**

 V

VEE—see **Equine encephalomyelitis**

V.M.D. (see also **D.V.M.**)—Veterinary Medical Doctor

VS—see **Vesicular Stomatitis**

vaccination (also "innoculation")—the artificial stimulation of antibody production or introduction of protective antibodies into the body.

vaccine—a preparation that promotes active immunity.

vagina—the canal between the cervix and the vulva; the birth canal.

valet—in racing the person who cares for a jockey's tack & riding equipment.

van—see **trailer**

variance—state of being different.

variation—deviation from standard type.

vascular—containing blood vessels.

vasodilatation [*vay-so-dih-luh-tay'-shun*]—dilation or enlargement of the blood vessels.

vaulting—equestrian gymnastics consisting of exercises and balanced movements on a moving horse.

vein—a blood vessel that carries blood toward the heart.

vector—see **carrier**

ventral—pertaining to the abdomen; down toward the belly.

verbals (also "cue" "command")—the voice commands used with horses: "walk," "trot," "whoa".

vertebrae—bones that form the spinal column.

vertical—1) the imaginary straight line that runs through the centers of the forelegs, demonstrating proper leg conformation; 2) in dressage, a line perpendicular to the ground from the horse's forelock to the nose; the nose must never come behind the vertical.

vertical fence—in jumping, an obstacle built straight up and down without spread.

vesicant [*ves'-ih-kent*]—an agent that causes blisters.

Vesicular Stomatitis (VS) [*veh-sih'-kew-lur stoh-muh-tie'-tus*]—a contagious viral disease of horses that is easily transmitted to humans and other animals.

veterinarian—a doctor trained and licensed to practice veterinary medicine on animals.

vetted out—examined, checked by a veterinarian.

viable [*vy'-uh-bul*]—living.
vice—a bad habit.
Viceroy—an elegant 4-wheeled formal carriage.
vigor—health, stamina, and resistance to fatigue, hardship, etc.
viral—pertaining to or caused by a virus.
virus—an agent causing disease in animals, plants, and humans.
vital signs—the respiration rate, pulse rate, and body temperature.
vitreous fluid [*vih'-tree-us*]—clear body fluid.
voice commands (also "verbals")—the vocal cues that a trainer teaches to a horse, suc
as "whoa" "walk."
volvulus [*vol'-vew-lus*]—a twist in the intestinal tract.
vulva—the external genitalia in the mare.

W

WEE—see **Equine encephalomyelitis**
walk—a gait having 4 beats; the horse's feet hit the ground in a specific order: right rea
right front, left rear, left front.
wall eye—blue, white, or colorless eye.
wall fence—in jumping, an oblong fence built of wood and painted to look like stone
wanderer foal—a foal that suffers from a convulsive syndrome as a result of lack c
oxygen during birth.
"ware"—abbreviation for "Beware" used to warn riders of branches, wires, etc.
warm-blood—term for horses of carefully mixed breeds, such as Trakehner c
Hanoverian; these animals are characterized by excellent athletic ability and siz
plus an even temperament.
warts—bump-like structures caused by papilloma viruses.
Warwick color—a very dark brown saddlery color.
washed out (also "washy" "lathered")—term for profuse sweating caused by nerves.
waxing—term used to describe the small drops of waxy material that form on the enc
of the mare's nipples very close to foaling time.
way of going—the manner in which a horse travels while working.
way of the ring—entering the ring to the right (counter-clockwise) unless otherwis
instructed.
wean [*ween*]—separating a mare and foal, so the foal cannot nurse its dam; usually dor
at 4-6 months of age.
weanling—a horse of either sex under the age of one year that is no longer nursing.
weaving—addictive stable vice where horse sways rhythmically back and forth, shif
ing the weight from one front leg to the other; caused by boredom.
weight cloth—in racing or eventing, a leather or felt cloth with pockets into which lea
is inserted for increased weight.
wethers—see **uterus**
Weymouth bit (also "bit and bradoon")—English riding bit consisting of thin snaffl
and a curb bit, each attached to its own headstall and reins.
Weymouth bridle (also "double bridle")—an English show bridle consisting of
cavesson, two headstalls, two bits, and two sets of reins.
wheel covers—on driving vehicles (especially in racing), covers to prevent anythin
from becoming entangled in the spokes of the wheels.
whip—1) a riding, driving, or training aid available in many styles and lengths; 2) i
driving, the name used for the person driving the horse; i.e. the Whip.
whip training—teaching a horse to respond at the touch of the whip.
whippers-in—in hunting, the individuals who assist the huntsman.
whirlbone lameness—see **trochanteric bursitis**

white—a true white haircoat is always over pink skin; most apparently white horses are actually mature grays, as their gray coat loses its pigment with age.

white face—see **bald face**

White Foal Syndrome—see **Lethal White Foal Syndrome**

white line—an irregular line around the hoof wall on the bottom of the foot that connects the horny sole with the horny wall.

whorl—an area on the haircoat where the hairs grow in a spiral or coil; can be used for identification similar to fingerprint whorls.

"win by a nod"—in racing, when the horse extends its head at the finish line.

"win by a nose" (also "short head" *British*)—in racing, the smallest advantage by which a horse can win.

windgall (also "wind puff")—a puffy swelling of the knee or fetlock joint caused by excessive strain.

windpipe—see **trachea**

windpuff—see **windgall**

windsucking—see **cribbing**

winging—faulty action in which the front foot swings in toward the opposite leg.

winkers—the term for blinkers on a driving bridle.

winking—term used to describe the quick contractions of the vulva that a mare uses to let the stallion know that she is receptive.

wire—in racing, the finish line.

withers—the highest point of the horse's back, at the base of the neck between the shoulder blades.

wobbler syndrome—incoordination and weakness of young horses.

wobbles—disease of horses characterized by incoordination, especially in the hind legs; thought to be a result of spinal cord compression, possibly inherited.

wolf teeth—small teeth that erupt in front of the first molars; they frequently interfere with a bit and are removed.

womb—see **uterus**

wood chewing—stable vice similar to windsucking/cribbing, but without air swallowing; thought to be caused by boredom or lack of salt or minerals in the diet.

working paces—in dressage, a trot or canter between collected and medium when the horse is not ready for collection.

wormer rotation—a system where a different dewormer is given at selected intervals in order to prevent the buildup of resistence by the targeted parasite.

wry tail—a tail that is carried to the side.

 Y

yearling—a horse between the ages of 1 and 2 years.

yellow body—see **corpus luteum**

young entry—in hunting, young hounds and young riders.

young riders—in combined training, exhibitors up to the age of 21.

youngstock—young horses, usually under the age of two and untrained.

youth—see **junior exhibitor**

 Z

zebroid—offspring from horse/zebra crosses.

zygote [*zye'-goat*]—a fertilized egg cell.

Bibliography

Adams, Dr. O.R. Lameness in Horses. Lea & Febiger, Philadelphia, PA., 1962.

Baker, Jennifer. Saddlery and Horse Equipment. Arco Publishing, Inc., NY, 1982.

Bowers, Mike & Steve. "The Kick Strap," DDM Reprints 1, Driving Digest Magazine, Brooklyn, CT; 1992.

Cabell Self, Margaret. The Horseman's Encyclopedia. A.S. Barnes & Company., Inc., Cranbury, NJ, 1963

Edwards, Elwyn Hartley, ed. Encyclopedia of The Horse. Peerage Books, London, 1985

Evans, J. Warren, ed. Breeding Management & Foal Development. Equine Research Pub, Tyler, TX, 1978.

Funston, Sylvia. The Kids' Horse Book. Greey de Pencier Books, Toronto, 1993.

Guralnik, David B. ed. Webster's New World Dictionary. Sec. Ed., World Publishing Company, NY, N.Y., 1972.

Hyland, Ann. Foal To Five Years. Arco Publishing, Inc., New York, N.Y., 1980.

Kellog, W. Craig. "Harnessing & Hitching the Single Horse." DDM Reprints 1, Driving Digest, Brooklyn, CT, 1992.

Kidd, Jane, ed. The International Encyclopedia of Horses & Ponies. Howell Book House, Macmillan Pub.,New York, N.Y., 1995.

Kidd, Jane. A Festival of Dressage. Howell Book House, Macmillan Pub., NY, 1986.

Kreitler, Bonnie. 50 Careers With Horses! Breakthrough Publications, Ossining, N.Y., 1995.

Leland, T.M., ed. The Miniature Horse in Review, Vol. 1-2. Small Horse Press, Ashland, OR, 1995-96.

Leland, Toni M. Show Your Mini. Small Horse Press, Ashland, OR, 1996

Leland, Toni M., ed. Getting Started With Minis, Small Horse Press, Ashland, OR, 1995.

Liestman, Linda. Welcome to the Wonderful World of Horses. Equine Graphics Pub Co., Ashland, OR, 1994.

Lower, Bill. "Starting The Driving Horse." DDM Reprints 1, Driving Digest, Brooklyn, CT, 1992.

Mettler, Dr. John J (Jr.). Horse Sense. Storey Communications, Inc., 1989.

Millar, George. "Training A Horse To Stand." DDM Reprints 1, Driving Digest, Brooklyn, CT, 1992.

Price, Steven D. Get A Horse! The Viking Press, Inc., New York, N.Y., 1974.

Price, Steven D. The Whole Horse Catalog. Simon & Schuster, New York, N.Y., 1985.

Strickland, Charlene. Tack Buyer's Guide. Breakthrough Publications, Inc., NY, N.Y., 1988.

Trapani, Jerry. Equine Hoof Care. Arco Publishing, Inc., New York, N.Y., 1983.

Wagoner, Don M., ed. Equine Genetics & Selection Procedures. Equine Research Pub, Tyler, TX, 1978.

Woodhouse, Barbara. Barbara's World of Horses and Ponies. Summit Books, NY, N.Y.,1984.

AHSA Rules for Combined Training. American Horse Shows Association, Inc., NY, NY, 1993.

CHA Composite Horsemanship Manual. Camp Horsemanship Association, Inc., Lawrence, MI, 1983.

Glossary of Horse Racing Terminology. Thoroughbred Racing Communications, Inc., http://www.equineonline.com, 1996.

"Fitting A Driving Bridle." DDM Reprints 1, Driving Digest Magazine, Brooklyn, CT, 1992.

"Glossary of Hunting Terms." Chronicle of the Horse, Middleburg, VA, 1992.

"Turning Out A Phaeton." Driving Digest Magazine, Brooklyn, CT, 1992.

We Want Your Input!
Help us make *Look It Up!* even better!

We welcome additions, corrections, or suggestions from our readers. If you know a "horsey" word that we have not included—or know an additional definition of any of the listed terms—or find an error or confusing definition, please feel free to contact us. Submissions must include two (2) substantiated sources for the proposed term.

If we accept your submission for inclusion in *Look It Up!*, we'll send you a complimentary copy of the next revision.

Just complete the form(s) below* and mail to Equine Graphics Publishing™ • 2425 Old Hwy 99 • Grants Pass, OR 97526-8765
*only one word per form, please.

‒ ‒

PLEASE PRINT OR TYPE

WORD or TERM _____

Source #1 _____

Title _____

Publication or Author _____

Publisher Name _____

Publisher City _____

Edition/Year of Pub._____ Page # _____

Source #2 _____

Title _____

Publication or Author _____

Publisher Name _____

Publisher City _____

Edition/Year of Pub._____ Page # _____

Your Name _____

Mailing Address _____

City_____ State _____ Zip+4 _____

We Want Your Input!

Help us make *Look It Up!* even better!

We welcome additions, corrections, or suggestions from our readers. If you know a "horsey" word that we have not included—or know an additional definition of any of the listed terms—or find an error or confusing definition, please feel free to contact us. Submissions must include two (2) substantiated sources for the proposed term.

If we accept your submission for inclusion in *Look It Up!*, we'll send you a complimentary copy of the next revision.

Just complete the form(s) below* and mail to Equine Graphics Publishing™ • 2425 Old Hwy 99 • Grants Pass, OR 97526-8765
*only one word per form, please.

PLEASE PRINT OR TYPE

WORD or TERM _____

Source #1 _____

Title _____

Publication or Author _____

Publisher Name _____

Publisher City _____

Edition/Year of Pub._____ Page # _____

Source #2 _____

Title _____

Publication or Author _____

Publisher Name _____

Publisher City _____

Edition/Year of Pub._____ Page # _____

Your Name _____

Mailing Address _____

City_____ State _____ Zip+4 _____